Change. Leader

CHANGE. LEADER

The changes you need to make first

Dr Jen Frahm

Jennifer Frahm Collaborations Pty Ltd

Melbourne, Australia

Contents

Acknowledgement of Country

I grew up on the land of the Yuwibara people, and now reside on the land of the Wurundjeri Woi Wurrung of the Kulin Nation. Aboriginal and Torres Strait Islander people are the oldest living culture in the world. They have been the traditional custodians of this land, which has never been ceded, for more than 65,000 years. I pay my respects to their elders past and present.

With gratitude

Ah community. No author gets to the end without a truly valuable community around them, supporting them, encouraging them, challenging them and urging them on. This book is in your hands because of that community.

It's in your hands because Donna Hardman triggered a realisation that there was still more to say that would be of value.

It's in your hands because Joanne King, Melissa Dark, and Julieanne Dimitrios provided critiques that made it a much better publication.

It's in your hands because Lena Ross, Jillian Reilly, and Melissa Dark are wonderful business partners and make me work smarter, more innovatively, and publicly.

It's in your hands because Kate Ware, Rebecca King, Amanda Boland, and Susan Lambe cheer on in the background and have high expectations of me.

It's in your hands because Kylie Lewis, Michelle Redfern and Oneka Jefferson-Cornelius stepped in to contribute on topics you need to know about but I don't have expertise in.

It's in your hands because once again I am ridiculously blessed to have a mother who is a professional editor and shows no sign of slowing down – thank you Leanne Frahm.

It's in your hands because my very valued clients have issues just like you.

With acknowledgment and gratitude,

Jen

Foreword

In a year where even the most future-ready leaders "had a moment", Dr Jen Frahm stepped up. Understanding conventional change tools needed a sharpen – a rethink – she got to work.

In *Change. Leader,* Jen provides space for personal reflection and learning as well as timely instruction for those who, having experienced a year like no other, understand that we must get back on our feet, refresh our skills and swiftly return to the business of change leadership.

Jen demonstrates why change leadership matters more than ever, explaining that storm is the new norm and that change leadership is both a noun and an instruction. She asks the question: *are you up for it?*

Recognising that there is no such thing as a perfect change leader, self-reflection, challenge and relentless learning are forgiven, indeed acknowledged, as our stock-in-trade.

I commend this book to public and private sector boards and executive teams, aiming to set the tone at the top, lead cultural and organisational change and be more responsive to an ever-increasing rate of transformation and disruption. It will challenge the way you think about change and leadership.

To those who wish to more effectively contribute to the important conversations of our time, be that standing up for gender and race equality or protecting our planet, this is our book and our shared challenge to put our new, or resharpened tools, to best use.

Donna Hardman FGIA FAMI GAICD MBA BCom

Non-Executive Director

Board Performance Coach

Change Leader

Introduction

If the first two decades of the 21st century have taught us anything, it's that uncertainty is chronic; instability is permanent; disruption is common; and we can neither predict nor govern events. There will be no 'new normal'; there will only be a continuous series of 'not normal' episodes, defying prediction and unforeseen by most of us until they happen.

Jim Collins & Bill Lazier,
Beyond Entrepreneurship 2.0

It's 2021. We are now facing collectively the most significant and disruptive changes in our careers, possibly lives. There is a clarion call for strong change leadership.

Are you up for it?

All of my work with leaders of organisations during change tells me one thing. If you want to lead change, you need to change yourself first. Every time.

There is no 'perfect' change leader. Even those who

are lauded for their outcomes and efforts in creating successful transformation recognise they are in perpetual change. Challenging themselves, learning new things, adapting, and growing.

The phrase 'change leader' is both a noun and an instruction.

Change. Leader.

You don't have much time, I understand that, and 2020 has left you weary and exhausted. This year, 2021, has started with an attempted coup in one of the largest democracies, a variation of COVID 19 that turns a curve on the graph of spread into a vertical line, and an escalation of public outcry on the matter of sexual violence against women by men in power; it does not appear that the scale of disruption is slowing.

So, this book is written in short segments. Consume in one hit, or dip in, absorb, let it settle, come back and take another chunk. It's your call.

Each chapter finishes with suggestions on what you can do to change your leadership approach to be more aligned with the future demands.

I want to be clear about the type of change you need to make. Success will not be measured by how big a change you make in your leadership of change; it will be in that you try. Any shift of the dial is a good one.

You will also find a reading list by way of the *Leader's Bookshelf* at the end if you want to go deeper.

But if the smallest thing that happens is that your subconscious absorbs these chapters and the lessons start to emerge in your leadership, you will be changing as a leader and being a better change leader.

65 Change Actions

This book presents 33 topics that represent areas for you to do differently or better. Each topic is followed with 2-3 change actions you can take to be a better leader of change.

My invitation for you is to consider each one on a line – where 'zero' is at one end, infinity at the other. As you work through each topic, mark on the line where you are. The metrics are subjective, relative and up to you – you might be a 5 or a 45. Think about what it would take to move you closer to infinity, not necessarily a great leap towards infinity, just progress.

This can be represented as a spider's map – see below.

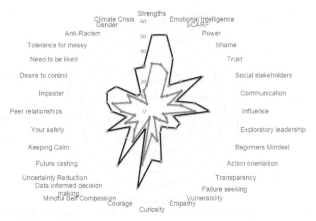

At the end of the book there is blank map for you to make notes of where you are at. This is a way of making sense of the changes you need to make personally, not a validated instrument of change. There is no definition of what zero is or what infinity is. I invite you to revisit this in six months' time after having time to repeatedly try the change actions and map how far you have shifted.

Why now? Why must you change?

We're entering a stage which has been described as late-stage capitalism. Late-stage capitalism is said to be characterised by increasing inequality, the rise of hugely powerful corporations, and absurd commercialisation of products and services (people will buy anything!)

Depending on which economic thinkers you follow, late-stage capitalism leads to either socialism OR fascism. Both have profound impact on organisational life and industry. The famous economist Joseph Schumpeter, in his well cited book *Capitalism, Socialism and Democracy*, describes how this leads to the cycles of 'creative destruction', and while the term 'creative destruction' has been most commonly used in reference to technology innovation, it means that the 'process of industrial mutation that incessantly revolutionizes the economic structure from within, incessantly destroying the old one, incessantly creating a new one.' There will be no return to 'normal'.

The storm is the norm[1]

What we understood to be disruptive prior was often largely visible and to some extent predictable and trackable. Futurists had an easier job of identifying signals. A significant proportion of disruption followed a technological determinist agenda – the new technology determined the innovation. Spotify replaced the music sales, Netflix obliterated the VHS / DVD market, and Uber overcame the taxi business.

The dependence on technology as a disrupter is largely based on the entrepreneurial zeal of the organisation, its financial position and willingness to be an earlier adopter. Disruption is often a choice. You can choose to disrupt; you can choose to respond to disruption.

The pandemic didn't follow that pattern. It provided an example of rapid large scale forced change with complex change impacts and took many by surprise. Not many 'Future Ready 2020' strategies had considered the likelihood of toilet paper being hoarded, airplanes grounded, and schools closed.

In 2020 we had a taste of what is to come.

Whether it be climate crisis induced, political instability inspired, or transformative social change the only thing that is certain, is that you will face into a significantly larger volume of disruptive change than organisational leaders have before.

This means the best of leaders, the most capable of leaders, those that will take healthy thriving workplaces into the future, will be the leaders who are accomplished at looking within and making repeated changes to the way they lead. This book will help you with that.

Onwards.

Notes

1. Credit goes to Lena Ross, my partner in the Agile Change Leadership Institute for this quote, so perfect for our times!

Chapter 1: Know thyself

To lead change, you need to go first. There is no way around this one. And the willingness to go first is enabled by how well you know yourself. In this chapter I share five components of self-knowledge that can help you lead change better and will be needed as you go forward to lead through continuing uncertainty.

Emotional Intelligence

To understand emotional intelligence is to know how our brains respond to threat *and* to behave in emotionally intelligent ways. At the risk of inflaming neuroscientists and dumbing down a complex organ, our brains can be considered as having three core functional areas. The prefrontal cortex is responsible for the cognitive thought, strategic thinking and higher order thinking. This takes up a lot of energy. Then there's the limbic system, which is the emotional processing component, and hosts the relational connections and responds super quickly. The third component is the reptilian brain which is responsible for keeping us alive (sleep, sex and hunger).

The advances in neuroscience and leadership in the last thirty years has resulted in much greater understanding of how our brains perceive volatility, uncertainty, ambiguity, and complex (VUCA) conditions. Broadly speaking, our brains privilege certainty and stability – and does so to keep us alive. When faced with sudden change, the limbic system (or emotional processing component) of our brain reacts at high speed, often generating what is known as the fight / flight / freeze response.

Our brain is also exceptionally good at noticing changes in the environment (error detection). When our brains perceive things are not quite right, they shoot a rapid impulse that stimulates the fight / flight / freeze component. In doing this it draws energy away from the pre-frontal cortex so it's quite normal to respond to immediate change and then say, 'I didn't think that through'.

A high degree of emotional intelligence permits us to counter that rapid fire response and temper the extreme stress response. Emotional intelligence (also known as emotional quotient or EQ) is the ability to understand, use, and manage your own emotions in positive ways to relieve stress, communicate effectively, empathise with others, overcome challenges and defuse conflict.

Two academics, Salovey and Meyer, first started doing research on the term coined 'emotional intelligence' in the early 90s. The original framework was:

1. Identifying emotions in the self and others.
2. Integrating emotions into thought processes.
3. Effectively processing complex emotions.
4. Regulating one's own emotions and the emotions of others.

Later, Daniel Goleman popularised the concept and broadened the application in his book 'Emotional Intelligence' published in 1995. Typically, people who cite Goleman's work refer to five elements:

- Self-awareness
- Self-regulation
- Self-motivation
- Empathy
- Social skills.

Emotional Intelligence continues to be central to leading change as repeated studies show that strong EQ reduces resistance, increases followership, and creates better teams.

However, it is fair to say that the forced disruptive change of a pandemic has tested everyone's EQ and amplified the need for it. I find it a little amusing how earnestly we used to throw around the term VUCA prior to 2020. Well, we certainly learnt very quickly how volatile, uncertain, complex and ambiguous things can be!

Our brains have been detecting a lot of errors in what was the normal of our lives. The need for empathy in managing distributed workforces became paramount, especially as employees had to work from home with little preparation and often in contested spaces (e.g., partners and children also requiring the same physical space).

Many organisational leaders, used to being quite resilient and with strong self-regulation, faced for the first-time feelings of doubt, despair and pessimism. You were being asked to care for your employees, care for your family, and were fearful that you had the capability to do this.

And with this fear came paralysis. Self-motivation was on the losing side of the equation.

The social isolation meant that social skills atrophied. On top of this you needed to be leaders who could deal with a workforce in grief, which is not typically part of your skillset. People mourned a considerable amount of loss last year and are continuing to mourn. Beyond the death toll of COVID19, your workforce lost opportunities to celebrate milestone events, lost connection with loved ones and friends, had partners who lost businesses, travel opportunities, jobs and schooling opportunities. There is still so much work to be done on how you lead with a grieving workforce.

The pathway forward for leaders beyond this loss is to reconsider how they use emotional intelligence in the day-to-day.

This could look like:

- Doing an emotional stocktake and acknowledging current emotional capacity is lower than usual.

- Responding to employee push back or reactivity with an assumption of positive intent.

- Extra time listening to employees to understand what is going on for them.

- Being intentional about what needs to happen to move forward, even if only a small step.

- Increasing connection by sharing how you are managing the challenges of the uncertain.

- Doubling down on creating psychological safety[1]

Here's an uncomfortable take on emotional intelligence. It's akin to the Dunning Kruger effect, the cognitive bias where people with low ability overestimate their ability. Leaders who think they have high emotional intelligence often lack it in spades[2]. A good way to test this is to reflect on, in the last three months, how many times have you wondered if you were connecting emotionally well enough with your employees. If the answer is only a few, then you could stand to shift the dial on this element of change leadership. With that in mind, here's the first of the *Change Actions* for you to consider – and note, a full list is at the end of this book.

Change Action #1: Sponsor the introduction of an organisational mindfulness program.

Change Action #2: Speak with a counsellor, coach or therapist about your emotional capacity to lead.

SCARF

For decades we went into change work based on a raft of psychological, sociological and communication theories. It wasn't until the advent of neuroimaging technology that we could actually see what went on in people's heads.

One of the main findings that has emerged from neuroimaging research is our brains seek to diminish threat and amplify reward – also known as the 'approach / avoid' response. This organising principle of our brain exists to keep us alive – what do we run from, what do we approach.

Dr David Rock and colleagues of the NeuroLeadership Institute developed a model that proposed that there were five elements most likely to create heightened arousal in the limbic system and generate a threat response (run from). When the emotional brain overheats, performance suffers, as does wellbeing.

These five elements were Status, Certainty,

Autonomy, Relatedness and Fairness – captured in the acronym SCARF™. It is worth considering how you respond to change with the SCARF™ lens. What we do know is the arousal state differs from person to person on each of these elements. I do not find a lack of certainty hugely problematic (fortunate, given my profession), I do struggle when autonomy is taken away, or fairness is violated. This means that I can be cavalier with elements of change that mean a lack of certainty – if it doesn't worry me, why should it worry someone in my team? But of course, that is not the case. The benefit of understanding *how you respond* to the SCARF elements is that it gives you insights into your biases – what you might over-emphasise or diminish in working with your people.

A threat to **status** is a change that makes us feel less good about ourselves. It may be a reduction of power, so a lowering of formal status, but it can also be triggered when you move into a new knowledge domain and you move from having mastery of a topic to being a beginner again. We talk later in the book about the qualities that are critical for you as tomorrow's change leader and these certainly mitigate the discomfort of a threat to status. As we emerge from 2020, we will all be in a position where we are doing things for the very first time. 'Unprecedented' has become one of the mantras for the year – and this means all of us will have threats to status in feeling like we don't quite know what we are doing.

A threat to **certainty** is triggered when we don't know what is coming next. This has been the greatest stressor for many people in 2020, where there has been great uncertainty in multiple domains. The brain privileges certainty and likes to fill in the gaps and connect the dots (often incorrectly). Strong change leaders develop a resilience and tolerance of uncertainty – but as in the example I used earlier, just because you are tolerant of uncertainty, doesn't mean that your people will be. Your leadership communication will need to maintain a dual focus, communicating what stays the same and at the same time, communicating what changes.

A threat to **autonomy** is any change that reduces your perceived control of your world. When political leaders institute lockdowns and restrictions, curfews and new rules, it is natural to react to that as a threat to autonomy. When people perceive they have some control over the change, they cope with it better. Uncontrolled change creates anxiety, fear, anger, and disengagement. Some leaders have reacted to employees working from home by installing activity tracking software, to be sure that their employees are working. This is a threat to autonomy, and you should not be surprised when those employees leave the organisation or underperform. If you want to be an effective leader of change, you need to keep your inner 'control freak' in check. The good news is many of the New Ways of Working coming through play to self-directed teams and high autonomy, and this should become normalised if you can let go of control.

A threat to **relatedness** is one where people struggle to trust others. In an environment of fear and uncertainty, people revert to tribal associations to feel safe (*people like us*). From a leadership perspective, to be effective in leading change you need to establish commonalities – people trust people they can relate to. As we emerge from 2020 and create a new way forward for our organisations, this will be a time of repair for relatedness. People are fractured, the intensity of fear and trauma experienced in the year has resulted in micro-communities that don't always relate well to others. Your role will be in reducing this threat to relatedness, finding the common threads that bind your people, and bringing that forward.

A threat to **fairness** is a change that is perceived as being inequitable and lacks justice. Research shows that people are much better with the bad news of change if the procedure is perceived to be just. For example, if you plan on downsizing you need to be clear on what the process is and the logic behind who is being downsized. The procedure of downsizing needs to be perceived as fair for it to occur effectively and for those who remain to continue to be productive.

It is important to recognise that what presents as a trigger for you may not be a trigger for others. You need to be thinking about what the threat triggers are for the people you need to lead in change. This self-awareness allows you to tailor your leadership change communication AND biases in decision making.

Change Action #3: Do a SCARF self-assessment to understand your biases and check with your team on their biases – are they in alignment?

Change Action #4: Review your leadership communications – are they equally weighted in effort to reduce threat to all five elements?

Strengths

A strengths-based approach to leadership is a core tenet of positive psychology, the area of psychology that focuses on flourishing rather than disfunction. We have known for some time that applying a strengths-based approach has innumerable benefits for the organisation and in leadership teams. Typically, we assess a leader's strengths using one of several validated diagnostic tools.

A leader who knows their own strengths and whose work plays to those strengths is usually a higher performer than one who is trying to focus on areas of improvement. This builds resilience in the leader. Working with your strengths makes you feel good. It releases the feel-good neurochemicals of dopamine and serotonin and this can assist with your emotional self-regulation.

While most of the research on strengths assessment tell us that strengths are inherently stable over time, most of that research using a *test – retest methodology* has been done in relatively stable times, not pre- and post-pandemic.

My belief is that coming out of a pandemic you will not have 'changed' your strengths, but you will have reprioritised the strengths you have and bought some lower order strengths to a higher use.

This can be explained by what's now known as the Strengths Profile model of strengths deployment. Initially designed by the Centre of Applied Positive Psychology (CAPP), it provides a way of making sense of the strengths you have. While typically applied to the Cappfinity Strengths assessment you can use the same concept with most of the strength's assessments available.

Strengths Profile identifies:

- Realised strengths that you typically perform well – ideally you can marshal these strengths when needed.

- Unrealised strengths – these are also performed well and once aware you can maximise and bring to the fore.

- Learned behaviours – these are things you do well, but they do not inherently energise you. It's advised to moderate their use.

- Weaknesses – these are things you do poorly, they exhaust you and can cause performance problems. Not surprisingly, you should minimise them.

So as an applied example of pre- and post-pandemic strengths, when I did the Cappfinity assessment in 2017 I found my top strength was 'Scribe' – not surprisingly, that was when I was finishing my first book *Conversations of Change: A guide to workplace change* which also fit with legacy and mission strengths.

2017 STRENGTHS PROFILE SELF-ASSESSMENT

Unrealised strengths	Realised Strengths	Weaknesses	Learned Behaviours
Order	Scribe	Adherence	Strategic Awareness
	Legacy	Incubator	Enabler
	Mission	Persistence	Emotional Awareness
	Judgment		Reconfiguration
	Action		
	Humour		
	Explainer		

Last November, my top strength was 'Innovation' – also not a surprise, as like most consultants and people who do workshops and speak for living, our revenue was smashed, and we had to innovate to re-imagine our service offerings. This meant I had to call forward my change agent and time optimisation strengths. Writing was still there, just not as important. The strengths in the Realised column were there earlier, but lower in order.

2020 STRENGTHS PROFILE SELF-ASSESSMENT

Unrealised strengths	Realised Strengths	Weakness	Learned Behaviours
Authenticity	Innovation	Adherence	Self-Awareness
	Change Agent		Rapport Builder
	Time Optimisation		Resilience
	Scribe		Listener
	Centred		
	Adventure		
	Spotlight		

The Cappfinity strengths assessment can be considered a functional strength assessment, focusing on what you do. The other dominant strength assessment in the market is the Gallup Clifton's Strength Finder, now known as StrengthsFinder20. This strengths assessment became popular in the early 2000s when the book *Now, Discover Your Strengths* was published by Marcus Buckingham and Don Clifton. Many of my realised strengths had reordered. They were still present, but the conditions of 2020 meant I was as consciously marshalling the strengths that would serve me best.

From this you can also identify what your strengths are in change. My top five strengths are: Strategic, Relator, Activator, Futuristic, and Maximiser. This means I am somewhat obscenely suited to change (good thing that!) – but even if you find that you have quite a different profile, your challenge now is to ask yourself – how do these strengths show up in change? It also shows you who you need as your support team. I work best with people who have strengths in execution.

The VIA Institute of Character takes a little bit of a different approach, focusing on your character. This will differ from the others in that it focuses on who you are as opposed to what you do. This doesn't make it preferable, in fact I would argue the leader who knows their functional strengths and their character strengths and can marshal these during disruptive times is in an excellent position.

Peterson and Seligman's book *Character Strength and Virtues (CSV)* is considered the character strength bible. CSV provides a detailed theoretical framework of the different types of character strengths and their implications in real life. Based on research, the book identifies six categories of human virtues that shape their persona. Each of the six divisions has multiple signature strengths that are unique. There are 28 strengths in total to consider.

These are:

- *Wisdom and Knowledge* – creativity, open-mindedness, curiosity, inquisitiveness to learn, broad perspective, innovation.

- *Courage* – bravery, consistency, personal integrity, energy, zeal.

- *Justice and Fairness* – leadership skills, good citizenship.

- *Temperamental Abilities* – mercy, forgiving attitude, modesty, self-control, rational thinking.
- *Humanity* – love, kindness, sympathy, care.
- *Transcendence and Peace* – gratitude, appreciation, hopeful, spirituality, self-enhancement.

The combination of these strengths varies from person-to-person and determine how they would think, feel, and act in different life situations.

With respect to my top five-character strengths, there's been a little movement post-pandemic. The five top strengths are all courage and change related, and perhaps the elements of my character that have permitted resilience and the moving through really challenging times.

Here's what I think is worth looking at as we emerge from the pandemic and face further disruption. The assessment of your strengths was probably last done when you were leading in what we would have called Business as Usual (BAU). They could be considered stability strengths, not strengths of disruptive forced change and crisis.

I would argue that it would be well worth revisiting your strengths assessment and reflecting on how did those strengths show up during the last year? Were there new strengths that emerged that you had not had the opportunity to demonstrate?

Second, the people you lead will be in a heightened emotional state as we go forward. They have been disconnected from friends and family. They have had to face career / job insecurity, concerns for loved ones, and the in many cases the despair for their children at the disruption to schooling. What an incredible gift it would be to use a strengths-based approach in leading them, building their self-confidence, firing off (dopamine), building trust and followership. This might be the perfect time to work with your Human Resources, Talent or Organisational Development teams to double down on leading with a strengths-based approach.

Change Action #5: Re-take your strengths assessment.

Change Action #6: Review the next three months. How can you marshal and maximise the strengths that will set you up for navigating continuing uncertainty?

Change Action #7: Reach out to each of your direct reports and provide some feedback on the strengths you have observed in 2020.

Relationship to power

While the previous three topics addressed self-understanding of how you respond to change and your strengths in change, the next two topics calls upon you to reflect on your relationship to power and shame. To start with, your ability to be an effective change leader will be in your ability to adopt new power principles and assume a 'power with' stance.

Traditionally, we taught about the work from French

and Raven in 1959 that the leader's sources of power could be based on six sources – reward, coercion, legitimate, expert, referent and informational power.

This was based on research that was 60 years old and yet under stress, and in circumstances where the work environment is changing out of control, we do see many leaders reverting to formal forms of power – reward, coercion and legitimate. In today's environment, these can be considered toxic forms of power and the gains will be short-lived.

They are driven by fear. The personal forms of power – referent (influence), expertise, and access to information can be considered healthier forms of power to display, albeit still dated.

These six forms of power that French and Raven propose relate to what research professor, speaker, and author Dr Brene Brown calls 'power over' and can be contrasted by 'new power', or 'power with', 'power to' and 'power within'.

Brene Brown and Power

In her book *Dare to Lead,* Brown describes the *Just Associated* framework of power use in the social justice field.

It introduces the terms 'Power with' 'Power to' and 'Power within'. These three forms of relating to power are positioned as the healthier way to lead with 'Power over' being a form of domination and oppression.

Brown states that aligning with 'Power over' is believing that power is finite, and that can be hoarded. 'Power over' is most commonly used to seed division. She argues that daring and transformative leaders share power with, empower people to, and inspire people to develop power within.

The power with / to / within may have originated from the social justice space, a field outside of traditional leadership domain but it is definitely a space that has faced significant complexity and uncertainty, not unlike leadership now.

A summary of the three power positions most applicable to leaders is provided on the next page and you are encouraged to reflect which forms of power you default to in times of stress.

Because of the legitimate authority that your role holds, we will return to this distinction many times in the book to illustrate how the shift from power over (possibly your default) to the sharing of power (with / to).

Type of power	Goal	Relationship to conflict	Strategies
Power over	Divide, devalue, destabilise, dominate	Drives conflict as a tool to retain power	Shaming, Bullying, Disempowering others, Gaslighting
Power with	Build collective strength based on mutual support, solidarity, collaboration and recognition and respect for differences, 'power with' multiplies individual talents, knowledge and resources to make a larger impact	Acknowledge diversity and disagreement, seeks common ground	Alliance and movement building
Power to	Individual builds self-worth and capability to make a difference	Withdraws from conflict and resigns themselves to current state	Nurture people's power to develop themselves

New Power

The other approach that you might want to consider is the shift in power from old to new. These are terms that come from Jeremy Heimans and Henry Timms' book *New Power*.

As they say in their Harvard Business Review article in 2014: '*Old power* works like a currency. It is held by few. Once gained, it is jealously guarded, and the powerful have a substantial store of it to spend. It is closed, inaccessible, and leader driven. It downloads, and it captures'.

Note the similarities with Brown's version of 'power over'.

'*New power* operates differently, like a current. It is made by many. It is open, participatory, and peer driven. It uploads, and it distributes. Like water or electricity, it's most forceful when it surges. The goal with new power is not to hoard it but to channel it.'

In their book, Heimans and Timms contrast the two with the following characteristics.

Old Power Values	New Power Values
Managerialism, institutionalism, representative governance	Informal, opt-in decision making, self-organisation, networked governance
Exclusivity, competition, authority, resource consolidation	Open-source collaboration, crowd wisdom, sharing
Discretion, confidentiality, separation between private and public spheres	Radical transparency
Professionalism, specialisation	Do-it-ourselves, 'maker-culture'
Long-term affiliation and loyalty, less overall participation	Short-term, conditional affiliation, more overall participation

The implications for leadership are considerable – and this very much represents *a power with* model of leadership. To be successful in navigating continuing and disruptive change is to employ more forms of new power.

It is important to note that your relationship to

power will inextricably be linked to your relationship with shame and so we look at this next.

Change Action #8: Audit your sources of power. If you look to peers who seem to be navigating the disruptiveness well, are they using power with or new power?

Relationship to shame

If the suggestion to move towards more forms of new power or power with / to within makes you recoil in discomfort or distaste, it might be that you have a bit of work to do on your need to control and your relationship with shame. It's not something we think about often in leadership, but it underpins so much of our dysfunctional behaviour – namely Bullying Blame and Bullshit.

2020 resulted in a series of 'shame storms' for organisational leaders. The unprecedented demands meant many were afflicted by feelings of:

- I'm not worthy, I'm an imposter.
- I'm not loveable, I'm not getting the attention I normally would.
- I'm not relevant. I don't have the skills to lead in this way.

When in a state of shame, our brain produces that heightened amygdala response (fight, flight, freeze). The survival response to the shame felt by leaders shows up as the three Bs: Bullying, Blame and Bullshit.

Fight becomes **bullying** and aggression.

Flight becomes **blaming** others and running away from the issue.

Freeze becomes covering up with **bullshit** and decision paralysis.

This behaviour becomes compounding as you know on some level you are acting out, and then feel more shame because of that which causes you to double-down on the bad behaviours.

Researcher and author Christopher Germer defines shame as the emotion that arises when we believe we are too flawed to be loved and accepted by others. He explains:

- Shame feels *blameworthy*, but it is an *innocent*.

- Shame feels *isolating*, but it is a *universal*.

- Shame feels *permanent* and *all-encompassing*, but it is *transitory*, like all emotions, and it is a burden carried by only *part* of who we are.

Shame is quite different from regret or guilt. As Germer notes above, shame is innocent, it is an uncomfortable feeling that we internalise when we believe we are not worthy, loved or relevant. Shame is experienced when *we* are hurting. Guilt is a response to something we have said or done that has caused harm *to others*. Regret is a response to something that we have done that inadvertently hurt another. Both guilt and regret are externalised harm, shame is internalised harm.

To translate this – we see leaders who think that their peers, the media, their employees are critical of them and they are not worthy of love. As I observed in the discussion on emotional intelligence, there has been significant expectation of leaders to have empathy for their employees. I also think though there has not been as much attention paid to the empathy needs of leaders trying to lead in the extreme disruption.

For many leaders, 2020 was a year when they were doing things for the very first time. It was the first time you had to run a company from a kitchen table, it's the first time you've had to deal with family in the background while running a leadership team meeting, it's the first time that you've had to shift your supply chains to a completely different way of working.

And when we do things for the first time, we are often very critical of ourselves. We think, 'I was not good enough, I should have done that better. What will people think of me? They won't like me anymore as a leader.'

And when we sit in self-judgment we sit in shame. This will cripple your ability to lead change. I referenced Dr Brene Brown's work on power initially but many of you will be more familiar with her with her global success with her Power of Vulnerability TEDx talk. What you may not know is that in continuing her research work on the topic of vulnerability and then shame, she has developed Shame Resilience Theory.

She talks about the biggest shame trigger being fear of irrelevance.

How many organisational leaders have charted a course of change out of fear of irrelevance and demonstrated in a kind of institutional 'me too-ism' – '*Company x is going agile, us too!*' Closer to home, I can't count the times I've used General Eric Shinseki's quote 'If you think you don't like change, you're going to like irrelevance even less'. It's a form of weaponizing shame really.

And so perhaps, unsurprisingly, we see leaders of change disengaging from the work that needs to be done, unable to make decisions, and acting hostile when provided with feedback. Shame creates paralysis because we don't know what we're going to do, we're embarrassed about the way we're doing it, it's not good enough, we won't do anything... Which doesn't help us with agility. We can sometimes react in anger and conflict and we lash out at people. And sometimes we avoid issues completely when we sit in shame.

Brown provides four steps to deal with 'shame screens', or the defence mechanisms of fight / flight / freeze:

1. Recognising the personal vulnerability that led to the feelings of shame.

2. Recognising the external factors that led to the feelings of shame.

3. Connecting with others to receive and offer

empathy.

4. Discussing and deconstructing the feelings of shame themselves.

For many of you, this will be the first time 'shame' has been discussed in context of leading change and may have surfaced uncomfortable feelings of recognition. The following change action is shared with empathy and compassion and will serve you well as a repeated exercise done in a gentle way. You are effectively carrying out the first two steps that Brown shares on how to work through defensive shame screens.

Change Action #9: Find a new journal that you can dedicate to exploring thoughts about shame. When you catch yourself in a moment of shame, write down what caused it, and what you think you would say to your best friend if they told you about it.

So, leader, are you up for it? This is where the real change begins – *within.* Personal change always precedes organisational change. This chapter has shown you five topics to start your change work in:

- Emotional intelligence
- Strengths
- SCARF [TM]
- Relationship to power
- Relationship to shame

A reminder, it is not expected you are starting from the beginning with these topics, by virtue of the fact that you are in a leadership position it can be expected that you already possess a high level of emotional intelligence, and understanding of strengths, neurobiology and perhaps some insight into power and shame. This is an invitation to broaden and deepen your personal insights, understanding and application in order to better lead continuing disruptive change.

In the next chapter we move from the internal perspective to the external and look to the changes you need to make in how you communicate and collaborate with others.

Notes

1. Edmondson and Laid define a psychologically safe workplace environment is one where employees do not fear retribution for taking interpersonal risks, such as speaking up, challenging the status quo, and engaging in congruent communication and collaboration for the greater good of the organization (Edmondson & Lei, 2014).
2. https://www.aim.com.au/blog/im-not-wrong-test-emotional-intelligence-vs-denial

Chapter 2: Collaborating and communicating through disruptive change

Melissa Dark

I hope it goes without saying that all the tools and approaches we discussed in Chapter One in 'Know thyself' can be used in consideration of others around you and deepen your understanding of your peers, direct reports, and partners in order to lead through continuing disruption.

However, your ability to navigate continued uncertainty as a leader will be amplified and strengthened if you do so collaboratively. This is part of leading with a 'power-with / new power' approach.

It's also a safety feature. You need to know who you can collaborate with to minimise the risk and disruption in the next era of work life. This means who can you:

- collaborate with on your leadership team.
- collaborate with in the organisation.
- collaborate outside of the organisation – partnerships, alliances, and networks.

This is something that my partner Melissa Dark in the Busting Silos program and I spend a lot of time working on, so this chapter is co-authored.

Trust

The ability to collaborate during uncertainty is highly dependent on the amount of trust developed. Trust is important because neurologically we are hard-wired to survive. If you recall the 'R – Relatedness' in the SCARF model in Chapter One, our brains make exceptionally fast decisions on whether you are part of our 'tribe' and can be trusted, or whether you are foe and likely to be a threat to our survival.

If someone determines that you are not to be trusted, they will expend a lot of energy in distancing from you. This makes collaboration nearly impossible. Silos emerge when groups decide that you are foe and cannot be trusted. Silos are protective devices for people seeking to survive. If you want to bust silos and collaborate more broadly, you need to build trust.

What does it mean to trust someone?

True collaboration requires individuals or organisations working together in the pursuit of mutual benefit, actively enhancing each other's capability. We like to refer to Arthur T. Himmelman's model of Relationship Hierarchy. Often, we think we are collaborating when we are only coordinating or cooperating.

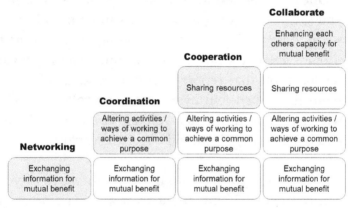

Himmelman states that true collaboration involves the four Rs – shared risk, reward, resources and responsibility. To reach the level of a 'collaboration' relationship according to Himmelman's definition, we need to create high levels of trust and communication and with that comes a significant risk.

So, what do we mean by that significant risk? In his book *The Thin Book of Trust*, Charles Feltman says:

'Trust is defined as choosing to risk making something you value vulnerable to another person's actions.'

Trust is built in a succession of small moments and

broken in an instant. We usually don't decide to trust someone in an instant. Although sometimes, for example during a crisis, we must, and certainly when large swathes of corporates moved to working offsite and remote working in as little as 11 days [1] when the COVID19 pandemic began, we did indeed have to trust in an instant.

One of the easiest ways to build up trust is to do what you say you're going to do. This can be both big and small things – for example, if you say you're going to provide feedback on a report within a week, provide feedback on that report within a week. It might not seem like much, but every time you follow through with your commitments, you add to your credibility and increase the likelihood of someone trusting you.

This means you need to be very protective of your commitments. Think about trust as a bank account. The ability to say no to things builds your trust credits. Every time you are honest, authentic and reliable, you add a credit to your account. The more credits you have, the better the trust you'll likely have built.

How can you practically go about building trust?

We mentioned above that trust is like a bank account and you need to build the bank balance with credits. But how do you go about doing that?

In the last chapter, we introduced you to Brene Brown, the professor researcher, leadership scholar, author and speaker who has studied trust. She has created an 'inventory' of the seven key attributes she has found that build trust over time. The inventory can be easily remembered with the acronym BRAVING.

Boundaries: You respect my boundaries, and when you're not clear about what's okay and not okay, you ask. You're willing to say no.

Reliability: You do what you say you'll do. At work, this means staying aware of your competencies and limitations, so you don't over promise and are able to deliver on commitments and balance competing priorities.

Accountability: You own your mistakes, apologise, and make amends.

Vault: You don't share information or experiences that are not yours to share. I need to know that my confidences are kept, and that you're not sharing with me any information about other people that should be confidential.

Integrity: You choose courage over comfort. You choose what is right over what is fun, fast, or easy. And you choose to practice your values rather than simply professing them.

Nonjudgment: I can ask for what I need, and you can ask for what you need. We can talk about how we feel without judgment.

Generosity: You extend the most generous interpretation possible to the intentions, words, and actions of others.

In a 2017 Harvard Business Review article called the *Neuroscience of Trust*, researcher Paul Zak shared that 'Compared with people at low-trust companies, people at high-trust companies report: 74% less stress, 106% more energy at work, 50% higher productivity, 13% fewer sick days, 76% more engagement, 29% more satisfaction with their lives, 40% less burnout'.

It strikes me the more that you can do to build trust now, the better you will be at finding safety in people to collaborate with and navigate uncertain futures.

Change Action #10: Conduct a BRAVING INVENTORY – how do you stack up?

Social stakeholders

A stakeholder is literally someone who has a stake in the outcome of your decision making. There are lots of different ways of defining and analysing stakeholders, but one of the most important first steps is ensuring you have the right people involved. In times of disruptive change this can be difficult because of the complexity of the situation and the costs of missing key stakeholders high.

Where leaders often go wrong in assembling the right group of stakeholders is that they default to the *tried and true*, those they have always considered or included. Truly volatile and uncertain working environments turn this approach on its head – new and emergent voices become especially important. In seeking to collaborate in this environment it is worth taking time to pause and ask yourself, 'Do I have the right people around the table?'

If the answer is 'no', then you need to do some work on mapping the ecosystem that is affected with a diverse group of people. You may be surprised how effective it is to use social media for stakeholder identification.

Celine Schillinger[2] of We Need Social, shares the story of how Sanofi, together with the Bill Gates Foundation, used social network analysis to build a social online community platform to connect stakeholders in the quest to eliminate Dengue Fever. Beyond the digital and technology side, the key to the success was identifying diverse pockets of expertise.

Taking this case study of success through social networks into the organisation, she notes:

'We need to engage in more than a conversation with diverse people across the world: we have to act together. But first, we need to listen to them actively, because they can tell us about our blind spots, they give us insights. We have to disseminate this insight throughout our organizations and create the conditions for serendipity to happen. We need to offer people exciting engagement opportunities, not just information.'

Chief Transformation Officer of the NHS and co-author of *Power of One and Power of Many*.[3] Helen Bevan affirms: 'We have to *strategize change from a social movement perspective.*' She explains with respect to her success in transformation in the health care setting:

'I was able to collaborate with people who could see the potential of bringing social movement thinking into health and healthcare improvements. I thought at that point in time, when you thought about change management or program management and you thought about social movement thinking they were two very distinct approaches. They came from different academic traditions. They operated in very different camps and people who worked in big programmatic change would never think about social movement thinking and people that use social movement thinking and were activists would never think about programmatic management. What we've seen over a period of time is actually the bringing of different ideas and different traditions together (and the success it creates). It's not one or the other. We have to work in ways that are about dealing with tensions and complexities and two different ideas often at the same time.'

Change Action #11: Map your social stakeholder network – who is missing?

Change Action #12: Note the communities you have access to that you could use to identify missing collaborative partners.

Your stakeholders' collaborative potential

Another way Melissa Dark and I like to think about stakeholders in the Busting Silos program is what we call *the Axis of Collaborative Potential*. This model requires thinking about the extent to which you trust a stakeholder as well as your familiarity and history with the stakeholder.

Our model plots stakeholders on two axes:

1. Familiarity – how well do you know the stakeholder? What has your past involvement with them taught you? What do you know of

their reputation? What credibility does their occupation, organisation or other external signifier provide?

2. Trustworthiness – do you have existing trust with this stakeholder? Have you worked with them before with good results? Do you have other references or recommendations that lead you to believe in their goodwill?

High Familiarity

The collaborators I have learnt not to trust	**My proven collaborators**
Worked with before and they have let me down	Proven collaborators in our workplace or industry

Low Trust ———————————————— **High Trust**

Collective reputation precedes them, driven by self-interest	Collective reputation precedes them, backed by credentialing bodies and ethics governance
The collaborators I don't know and don't trust	**The collaborators I don't know but do trust**

Low Familiarity

© Melissa Dark and Dr Jen Frahm 2020

Low trust / high familiarity

- Suppliers you have worked with before, but who did not deliver good results.

- Members of your team, organisation or the community whom you have worked with before, but who have proven to have conflicting agendas or motivations.

- Anyone you know well but through past experience have learned not to trust.

Approach: Instigate boundaries and do not engage.

Low trust/low familiarity:

- Stakeholders you are working with for the first time and whom you have reason to distrust – either due to their history, occupation (e.g., politician, real estate agent) or reputation.
- Stakeholders you need to work closely with whom you have only peripherally been engaged with in the past.
- Stakeholders whom you need to work with, but you have no common connections who can vouch for their credibility.

Approach: Take small steps – trust but verify, minimise risk by size of activity.

Low familiarity/high trust:

- Stakeholders who are new to you but who come with references – recommendations from other people you trust, or there are other reasons that encourage you to trust them.
- Stakeholders in occupations that engender trust (e.g., healthcare, emergency services, educators).

Approach: Verify then trust. Keep engagements minimal

until such time you are aligned with references and they increase familiarity.

High trust/high familiarity:

- People you have worked with before and have found to be trustworthy – proven collaborators.

Approach: Provide clear guidelines and vision and then let them loose.

It's important to note that we're not making blanket judgements on these professions. The Edelman Trust Barometer [4] identifies that there are some professions that are inherently judged as less trustworthy than others – and while trustworthy politicians and real estate agents, etc., absolutely do exist, these people face a disadvantage in having to prove their trustworthiness due to an overall community sense of distrust. On the flipside, people in trustworthy occupations (e.g., healthcare) can be given unwarranted levels of trust for the same reasons.

The point here is that in leading through continuing disruption, much of the uncertainty may come from the level of familiarity you have with those you might need to collaborate with. If you have used the social stakeholder mapping approach described by Schillinger and Bevan, it is highly likely that you are coming across stakeholders that are unfamiliar with you (and this can even apply IN your organisations). You're invited to refer to the approaches in *Axis of*

Collaboration we teach in the Busting Silos program on how to deal with that.

Change Action #13: Draw up the axis of collaborative potential and note one stakeholder in each grid to test the approaches.

Communicating with others

Leadership communication during volatile, uncertain, complex and ambiguous environments is often intuitive. We speak and issue communications at speed. The ability to think more strategically about how you approach communicating with your stakeholders and your collaborators adds value in many ways. It can require a bit of up-front investment in time, but typically it saves time in the end by reducing confusion, re-work, and potentially calamitous misunderstandings.

Communication objectives

As you lead through disruption, you will no doubt have a direction if not an objective that you wish to achieve. We're going to encourage you to pause and consider what your communication objectives are in this regard.

There is a basic question at the heart of all communication strategies.

What do you want people to know, think and do?

What do you want people to know?

This is often as far as people get when they think about

communication. And it's definitely an important consideration. What do you want people to know about your project, its goals, and the results or outcomes you are striving towards? What do you want people to know about the process you will be undertaking to get there?

This objective is about information. It's about the facts and details you need people to know about. The who, what, when, where, why and how of what is happening.

You've likely already thought about it, but it's worth giving it further consideration. Is the information people need to know the same for every stakeholder or stakeholder group? Should you be tailoring information so that you don't overwhelm some, or under-inform others?

How are you going to manage the information vacuum? One of the hallmarks of disruptive change is that you rarely have all the information at the time you are having conversations. Waiting until you have perfect information is not an option.

What do you want people to think and feel?

This objective is about attitudes. How do you want people to feel about the direction you are taking? If someone else asked them about what it's like to work with you as a leader, what would they say?

Attitudes are important because they become an indicator of successful behaviour change. Once the change has embedded, the attitudes shift. A good way to approach this is to think of a list of adjectives you'd like people to use when talking about your direction. Once you have the list, you then consider how your communication is going to encourage those feelings with your stakeholders.

This is especially important as we move further away from 2020 and people are to a large extent traumatised by the year. How will you help them feel optimistic, empowered, enabled and hopeful? It's worth spending some time on this and really scrutinising the language you use to ensure that you don't embed your language with fear-based messaging. As an example, consider the difference between signing off your leadership communications with:

'Until next time, keep safe.'
'Until next time, stay well.'

The first sentence primes you for danger and puts you on high alert, the second sentence affirms your good health, and with that comes and implicit congratulations of the things you are doing right.

Your word choice will be incredibly important in setting the tone of a workplace that can grow, adapt, flex and change.

What do you want people to do?

This objective is about behaviour. Typically, you have a behavioural objective when facing into continued change. It could be a simple new work process or something that has a significant impact on the way they do their jobs. If behavioural change is a core outcome of your collaboration and communication, you will need to spend more time planning and designing your approach or working with an expert in this field.

You might have already realised this, but the difficulty of success increases as you move from *know*, to *think* and to *do*. Getting people to know about something is relatively easy. Changing attitudes and behaviours can be exponentially more difficult. We would argue for encouraging people to experiment, practice the doing, and then you find that the 'thinking' catches up when faced with the personal experience and proof.

Message platform

A 'message platform' (sometimes also called a 'message map') is a concept borrowed from marketing. In marketing it is critical that the messages issued by a brand (whether advertising or other material) are congruent with the brand identity and promise. A message platform is how marketers create their messages and ensure alignment. These become important in providing a strategic touch point to your continuing communications. A quick Google will show you that marketing message platforms can be extremely complex, and we typically don't need to get into that level of detail when we're planning communication for collaboration. For our purposes, we like to focus on three main elements:

Vision:

Don't be put off by the name. By 'vision' we mean an overarching statement that sums up your collaboration effort. Having this stated explicitly in words can be helpful in guiding your work and ensuring alignment back to your true purpose.

Key messages:

Key messages are the simple, core, takeaway messages that you need your audiences or collaborators to know. Where most people go wrong with key messages is in thinking that key messages must tell the *entire story* of a project or process. While that narrative is important, that's not what key messages are about. There's debate about exactly how many key messages you should have. But we'd advise keeping it to no more than five. These are the fundamental underlying takeaways that you need people to remember and understand. You might find that three key messages align with your Know, Think, Do objectives (but not always).

Yes, messages might change over time as you move from one phase to the next of navigating disruption. But if you think they need to change drastically then you might have fallen into the trap of confusing narrative and key messages. Key messages should be relatively stable throughout the life of your work.

Proof points:

Your key messages need to be backed up by proof points – that is, the facts and data that you are going to use to support your message. This helps you get clear on how your key messages translate into the real world. It's easiest to demonstrate this with an example:

Example key message:

We need to be thinking about how our company adapts to changing government policy on workplace health and safety.

Example proof points:

- We have a duty of care to our people.
- Legislative updates will now have a reduced time to comply with new mandates.
- There will be fines of up to $100,000 given to companies who do not comply.

An executive Melissa worked with earlier in her career used to say that he kept his key messages document on the wall of his office. Whenever he was asked to approve a piece of communication, he'd compare it to the key messages and if he couldn't see at least one of them reflected in the piece in front of him, he wouldn't approve it. Could you apply something similar in the way you approach your communication to stakeholders?

Change Action #14: Create a message platform for the next three months.

Change Action #15: Review the think / act / do framework with a change that is immediately important to you.

On influence

Joseph Wong says, 'Influence is our inner ability to lift people up to our perspectives.' Collaboration is dependent on our ability to share perspectives, and so influencing is a critical skill.

The idea of using communication to influence others' knowledge, attitudes and beliefs is not a new one. It probably existed when one cave dweller tried to get another cave dweller to go hunting together! But one of the historical figures that's most known for his work in this space is Aristotle.

Aristotle wrote in *Rhetoric* about three elements of a message that combine to form persuasive communication.

They are:

Pathos	Appeal to emotion
Ethos	Appeal to character, respected and credible sources of information
Logos	Appeal to logic; rational, statistics- and information-based

If you've ever done any kind of organisational profiling (like Human Synergistics' LSI, etc.) or done any kind of education training, you'll have learned that people have a range of styles and preferences in the way they approach and process information. Some people need cold, hard facts before changing their mind on a topic, others will be persuaded by a passionately told story.

Aristotle's thinking, and our more recent discoveries around human and organisational psychology, show that we need to consider a rounded approach to our messages and appeals. For many of us, this means thinking about our own style. If you're the kind of person who is won over by an emotional and well-told story, you might need to be careful that your communication includes enough logic and facts to appeal to those with other styles (and vice versa).

Crafting messages that will have cut-through with your audience

Chip and Dan Heath's book *Made to Stick* was a smash hit when it came out more than 10 years ago, and it has stayed relevant since. The book looked at the crucial components of messages that 'stick' with an audience and broke down how to design 'sticky' messages.

Made to Stick argues that good messaging that resonates with audiences contains six key elements:

1. **Simplicity** – Cut to the core of what you are trying to get across (remember people are

currently and will be in a state of overwhelm for some time).

2. **Unexpectedness** – Something about the message surprises us. Think about your favourite joke or comedy routine, or an advertisement that you remember from the TV – it's likely that it's memorable and enjoyable because it includes an element of surprise.

3. **Concreteness** – The easiest way to understand 'concreteness' is by what it *isn't*: remember the last time you vagued-out in a conversation because someone was using jargon or buzz-words that you didn't fully understand? Concreteness isn't necessarily dumbing things down, it's making sure you use language that is shared, expressed in ways that everyone can grasp.

4. **Credibility** – Credibility is Aristotle's *ethos* and *logos*. It's not only having a credible source for the message but using facts and figures in a way that lends authenticity to your story.

5. **Emotional** – Use personal appeals to help people understand the importance of the message. Like Aristotle's *pathos*, this is where you try to get people to not only understand what you're saying, but to care about it too.

6. **Story** – For the Heath brothers, story is where messages move from *Know* and *Think*, into *Do*. *Made to Stick* argues that by using

storytelling we can empower people to take action from an idea.

In the last few years storytelling has become a popular tool in leadership and organizational communication. Storytelling encapsulates both Aristotle and *Made to Stick*'s key focus. To communicate with influence and cut-through, a message has to make your stakeholders:

- Pay attention (by including something unexpected)
- Understand and remember it (by being concrete and easy to grasp)
- Agree/ Believe (by being credible and supported by facts and a trustworthy source)
- Care (by including an emotional appeal)
- Be able to act on it (by including a simple 'call to action' typically presented through story)

Structuring your approach to *Conversations of Influence*

While many of the opportunities you are having at the moment to influence are adhoc and in the moment, there are equally many opportunities to be considered in your approach.

We use a very simple framework we call Conversations of Influence that outlines three key phases with important steps in each.

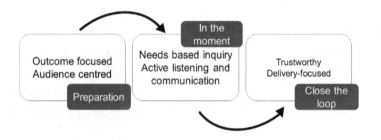

1. Preparation

- Outcome focused – get clear about what you're trying to achieve from this interaction. Go back to your Know, Think, Do objectives. What information, feelings and actions do you want to leave your stakeholder with?

- Audience centred – be sure you know as much as you can about this stakeholder going into the meeting. What have you learned from others about this stakeholder?

- Messages clarified – get your messages solid and clear. How have you applied pathos, logos and ethos and the lessons for sticky messaging to what you need to present?

2. In the moment

- Needs-based inquiry – make sure that you have the stakeholders' needs central to your conversation, if you get off track return to those needs.

- Active listening and communication – listen actively during the meeting to ensure you're hearing what's really said. Get curious and ensure your own agenda or preconceptions don't get in the way. Remember *Ethos*, *Pathos* and *Logos* while you talk.

3. Closing the loop

- Be trustworthy – continue to build trust by doing whatever it was you said you were going to do in the meeting. Follow up. Issue feedback on reports on time, and as promised.

- Delivery-focused – keep your stakeholders updated on how you are delivering on what you said you would. Let them know immediately of any delays that are likely.

Change Action #16: Use an upcoming change that you are sponsoring and review your power of influence using Aristotle's Pathos, Ethos and Logos.

Change Action #17: Use an upcoming conversation that you need to influence and map out the key components of the Conversations of Influence model

The 2021 Edeleman's Trust Barometer indicated that the only group who had achieved increased trust was business leaders. Government, media, NGOs have all lost trust as a result of how they managed communication and actions during the pandemic. The stakes are indeed high, but the way forward is clear. The Edelman's Trust Barometer report closed out with:

- Business must embrace its expanded mandate and expectations, with CEOs leading on a range of familiar and unfamiliar issues. It's important to take meaningful action first and then communicate about it.

- Societal leaders must lead with facts and act with empathy. They must have the courage to provide straight talk, but also empathise with and address people's fears.

- Provide trustworthy content that is truthful, unbiased, and reliable.

- Institutions must partner with one another to solve issues. Business, government, media, and NGOs must find a common purpose and take collective action to solve societal problems.

Your ability to collaborate with others to solve the problems ahead will be paramount. And you need to know the 'others' and the best way of engaging and communicating to do that well. This chapter invites you to look again at the following topics in order to ensure you are best placed for continuing disruptive change:

- Trust
- Collaboration
- Social Stakeholders
- Communication
- Influence

Now is not the time to be complacent with old ways of

communicating and engagement, nor to bolster silos. It might also be the time to consider new beliefs and ways of thinking that might assist you. The next chapter: Mindsets Matter will help you with that.

Notes

1. https://www.mckinsey.com/business-functions/strategy-and-corporate-finance/our-insights/how-covid-19-has-pushed-companies-over-the-technology-tipping-point-and-transformed-business-forever
2. https://weneedsocial.com/blog/2014/10/2/forget-social-networks-think-social-impact
3. https://www.england.nhs.uk/improvement-hub/wp-content/uploads/sites/44/2017/11/The-Power-of-One-the-Power-of-Many.pdf
4. https://www.edelman.com/trust/2021-trust-barometer

Chapter 3: Mindsets matter

Lena Ross and Jillian Reilly

> Thoughts are behaviours we haven't learned to observe yet.

> B.F. Skinner

When we talk about 'mindsets', some people struggle with what it means; is it fixed? Can you change it? How does it form? I would argue that a mindset represents a set of filters, attitudes and beliefs that process information to guide how you operate.

Your mindset is shaped by these influences that you believe to be true and have a good dose of certainty to them to you. This attachment to certain filters, attitudes and beliefs then influences what the data is that you search for when trying to answer a question. The degree of confidence you have in your beliefs creates a self-confirming cognitive bias of data seeking, and with this, creates additional stability to the mindset you hold (the fixedness).

While some claim that you cannot change a mindset, I would argue just because your set of filters, beliefs and attitudes is established, they are not set in stone. You can shift those beliefs and attitudes, indeed change them completely, depending on the importance of the change and the proof provided to you as the importance of the change.

At some point, it gets more difficult to find data that supports a pre-existing attitude, and the certainty in your belief may erode as the external environment changes.

Mindset change occurs either naturally, organically and introspectively, that is, over time you change your beliefs and attitudes about an idea, a concept or situation. Or you are guided through that mindset change deliberately with the help of a professional or a development program conducted by your organisation.

What's important to recognise is that you don't change a mindset by enrolling people in a one-day event. Changing mindsets take the same approach as any other change in the organisation. You need to be aware of the alternative, you need to understand why the alternative is important, you need to have opportunity to try to think and lead using those beliefs and attitudes and build confidence in their efficacy.

Once you see benefits in the newer beliefs and attitudes (for you), you become committed to that mindset.

There are two important mindset shifts needed to navigate the next era of our work lives, an *exploratory* and an *agile* mindset. Your mindset will be one of the most important contributors to success, and so if your mindset is not setting you up for successful navigation of relentless change and new frontiers, then you do need to do something about it!

Exploratory mindset

With Jillian Reilly

When the future workspace continues to be unknown, unforeseen and unprecedented, it is fair to say we are leading at the edge of a changing world. Every time our external circumstances change and embed as a sustainable change (e.g., not just a blip or a spike or something fleeting) we need to adapt as an evolutionary response. The navigating of novelty as a way of doing business is frontier work!

Navigating the new and novel is not technically unprecedented. Explorers have been doing it for thousands of years. This is why my business partner in the Big Bounds program Jillian Reilly and I turned to analysing how explorers deal with the unknown as a way of considering how leadership needs to change.

Jillian is not new to exploring, having worked with

NGOs and community groups in South Africa after moving there to monitor the elections for the United Nations. She subsequently then moved to Zimbabwe to start an HIV / AIDS program at the height of the country's epidemic.

A rose by any other name?

How does exploratory leadership differ from adaptive, servant or agile leadership? It's a good question. We think it is a nuanced but important shift and, as so many have struggled to make the transition to agile or adaptive, it may be that *exploratory* resonates more with some.

For us, the difference between exploratory leadership and the other styles is the willingness to accept that the future is both unknown **and** full of possibility.

An explorer takes a sanguine view that deep uncertainty carries with its boundless possibility ... if someone is willing to do the frontier work. Rather than regarding future change as a threat to be managed – which brings with it the uncomfortable neurobiology of 'fight, flight or freeze' – the Explorer treats change as an opportunity to 'learn, adapt and create'.

For the exploratory leader, maps that sketch out the business terrain are as, if not more, important than plans detailing future actions. In this way, the skillsets and approaches of an exploratory leader are different to those who believe they are shepherding towards a largely defined future.

Navigational skills come to the fore: reading the contours of the business landscape, recognising landmarks, and being able to zoom into immediate details and zoom out to the horizon. By necessity, explorers' toggle between presence and foresight – what's beneath their feet and what they cannot see.

Explorers know it's not a race

In contrast to the high-velocity changes of many of our contemporary leadership models, exploratory leaders persist in the face of discomfort and even failure. They tap into embodied wisdom and compare that to the available objective data. They persevere rather than pivot. They understand that curation and creation are more valuable than control.

We created this table to explain how Exploratory Leadership differs from other contemporary leadership models such as Adaptive Leadership, Servant Leadership and Agile Leadership. We see that each of these leadership models are represented by a specific mindset, and the leaders that enact the style of leadership have qualities they bias or highlight.

We also see a marked difference in the relationship of independent action versus collaborative activity and the speed of change in each of these models. These might be a useful way for you to assess what is

the relative mix of leadership models in use in your
leadership team.

Style of Leadership	Objective	Mindset	Qualities to highlight	Independence v collaboration	Speed of Change
Adaptive	To survive changes external to the organisation	Evolutionary	Emotional intelligence, Fairness. Lifelong learning	Facilitation of people	Adapt or die – improvises relentlessly
Servant	To steer changes internal to the organisation	Other focused – in service	Empathy, Humility, Encouraging	Collaborative – serving others needs	Dependent on those you serve
Agile	To get increase speed of organisation output – competitive advantage	Faster means success	Curiosity, Courage, Empathy	Teamwork is the dreamwork	Pivot or perish (#failfast)
Exploratory	To find a different way forward	I wonder what's next?	Curiosity, Courage, Creativity	I lead first to explore, then we go together	Persist with prudence

Go further than you would, no further than you should

Daryl Conner (*Leading at the Edge of Chaos* and
Managing at the Speed of Change)

The notion of *persisting with prudence* is an important
one – exploratory leaders are good at risk-mitigation
and establishing boundaries. They balance
independence with collaboration. Explorers rely
heavily on experts and supporters to establish
psychological and organisational safety boundaries.
There's no climbing rock faces without harnesses. No
treks without water and compasses. Think more
intrepid than rogue.

It's an operating system, not an interface

Exemplars are difficult to find as much of this is evidenced in 'inner world' characteristics, known only to the individual. Certainly, there are interviews, public talks, and biographies of people like Brene Brown, Julia Gillard, Michelle Obama, Prince Harry and Elon Musk that show evidence of exploratory leadership.

We don't have to necessarily like them, indeed there are many infamous leaders who have explored new ground, but it is instructive to look at the ways they have forged ahead with creating change at the frontier of industry, political systems, knowledge domains and institutions.

Signs you're an exploratory leader

If by this point of the chapter you are wondering if you are an Exploratory leader or have characteristics of the explorer, here's a non-exhaustive list of what we have determined shows up in those that do explore new frontiers.

- You have invested time in understanding the mind-body connections and are attuned to your physical state and the feedback it provides you – breathing, tension.

- You are a continuous learner, curious and protective of time to develop.

- You deliberately curate ideas, insights, data and self-discoveries. You're actively shaping and applying your learning.

- You are a boundary-keeper – you exercise prudence in your personal boundaries and your organisational boundaries.

- You are courageous and this informs your independence, you don't need others to make a stand, and it also backs your likelihood to persist in a course of action.

- You are creative and expressive – in some aspect of your life there is an aptitude to creative expression, and this is the place you exercise playful exploration.

- You're comfortable with conflict – you'd prefer it to be creative and constructive though!

In our work that we do with leaders on exploratory mindsets, it's important to note that the goal is not to make every leader an exemplar of an Explorer. It is useful though to think of the composition of your leadership teams and your hiring priorities, and talent development.

Are you hiring for, promoting for, developing these elements of leadership? If you want to be leading through continuing disruption, these are a clue to the vital composition of your leadership teams.

In Chapter Two I introduced you to Celine Schillinger. Celine is founder and CEO of We Need Social, Knight of the French Order of Merit, French Businesswoman of the Year (2013), an IABC Gold Quill

Winner and five times award winner in 2017 alone and an extraordinary role model for exploratory leadership. On the topic she says:

'My path is really marked by exploration, by doing different things, by trying different things. It has been really the common thread across all my professional life, probably. While others choose specialization, which is good, we need specialists, but if you have an organisation entirely run by specialists then you have people thinking in their own narrow world, if you wish, which is not adapted to the diversity, the complexity, the speed of change of the world today. So, we need more people working with those specialists but able to cross boundaries, able to connect different worlds.

Going beyond some boundaries that are familiar, reassuring, testing new things. It is dangerous, it is uncomfortable. Very often when I was about to change direction and was challenged, I could not explain what I was doing. The consistency is often retrospective, but there is one, it is possible. It is such an amazing fuel, energy. It gives the sense of continuous growth, which is to me the essence of life, being alive.'

She cites David Le Breton, an anthropologist from the book: *Adventure: the Passion of Detours.*

'Adventure takes place outside of routine or marked routes. The exultation it arouses comes from this razor's-edge path that always gives the adventurer an acute conscience of being alive ... Rather than an event, adventure is an advent in the sense that its duration gives birth to a new person transfigured by circumstances foreign to dullness'.

She explains: 'Exploration and being alive. We cannot waste what we have, what we have been given by chance. We have only one life, we cannot waste it. It is our responsibility to explore it to the fullest.'

I must agree with Celine, there is strong reason to argue that when it comes to changing our mindsets as leaders – if not now, then when?

Change Action #18: Reflect on your childhood explorations; if there was one element of how you used to explore as a child that you could bring forward tomorrow, what would it be?

Change Action #19: Make a list of explorers that you admire. What of their behaviours could you model yourself on?

Change Action #20: Enrol in an art class and spend some time being creative

Agile Mindset

With Lena Ross

When we think about navigating relentless change, the word agility often comes up and we measure ourselves on our ability to be nimble, to pivot, to adapt. The extent to which we can do this often relies on an agile mindset.

Leaders with agile mindsets probably saw the pandemic as an accelerator more than a negative disruption. When things are disrupted it's easy to bring in change: Go, go, go!

At last year's Australian-Israeli Innovation Summit,

Kelly Bayer Rosmarin, CEO of telecommunications company Optus, spoke of how they were forced to expand their experimentation with chatbots on all channels when overnight their contact centres struggled with staff being sent to work from home. 'Release the bots! Let the machine learning do what it's designed to do.' The forced experimentation has resulted now in 84% of all service inquiries being handled by chatbots in digital channels[1].

This preparedness to experiment is a hallmark of an agile mindset in leadership and aligns with Lena Ross's (author of *Hacking for Agile Change*, and co-founder of the Agile Change Institute) definition of agile mindset: 'It demonstrates the ability to recognise failures and challenges as opportunities for learning and improvement, along with resilience to evolve and adapt to make changing requirements.'

In her book, Ross offers a model that explains why we go so wrong with introducing agile in organisations. Much of the training that we do when we're seeking to create more agile organisations really focuses on the practices and the behaviours.

The training focuses on the *doing agile*, what you *do* and *deliver* and how you *act*. And the reason why we get tripped up on that, why we're not always so successful, is that we actually have to focus on mindset first. We can't be successful with large scale organisational agility if we are relying on old mindsets.

Four shifts

Lena and I propose that there are four shifts that we need to make to have an agile organisation.

All of these are likely to be difficult and challenging for many leaders as they deviate from what has been privileged, rewarded, and taught in the past. They also tap into our relationship with power, especially when we are relying on a *power over* approach.

Shift 1: From expert mindset to beginner's mindset

The first shift is that of an expert mindset to a beginner's mindset. In the past, whether it be in the family, the school or the workforce, you have been rewarded and promoted for your expertise and being clever at what you do. However, if we are truly operating in unprecedented times, how can we hope to have experiences and assumptions that will address those unprecedented times?

To be better able to handle the disruptiveness of our environment now we need a beginner's mindset because your prior assumptions and your experience are going to get in the way and be an anchor that could stop you moving forward.

A beginner's mindset is best exemplified by the way that young children think, constantly seeking other ideas and feedback, suspending judgement and asking that most perfect of questions 'But why?' The beginner listens deeply and asks, 'How might we?'

In the beginner's mind there are many possibilities, in the expert's mind there are few.

Shunryu Suzuki

One of the easiest ways to move into a beginner's mindset is to use the work of Carol Dweck on growth mindset. She talks of the power of the word 'yet'. When we add the word 'yet' to the end of our sentences, we find that we create opportunities to think about things in a different way. There's a real permissiveness in the word 'yet'.

I can't do this, *yet.*
This doesn't work, *yet.*
I don't know, *yet.*

That little word opens amazing opportunities for us when it comes to thinking differently. It can also be a supportive way to lead your people and peers; catch them saying things that shut down opportunities and just add the term yet to that sentence.

Change Action #21: Create a team challenge to catch each other using sentences that could benefit from the word 'yet'. Keep a tally and reward the person who caught the most in a specific time frame.

Shift 2: From perfection to done.

The second shift is 'done is better than perfect', which means you need to let go of perfectionistic tendencies. One of the challenges with perfection is that it can often create paralysis, we stop what we're doing because it's just not good enough based on our internal expectations of what is perfect. The definition of perfection is always subjective and rarely achieved.

There is seldom an objective measure of what is perfect because it depends on how you see perfection. If we are stopping what we are doing, we're not being agile.

When we shift our mindset to placing a value on what is 'done', we open opportunities for feedback and collaboration from other people – we ask the question 'Is this done yet?'

So again, we're bringing 'yet' back into the conversation. It aligns to the progress principle which rewards small wins. As Amabile and Kramer say in their 2011 HBR article on *The Power of Small Wins*,
'Of all the things that can boost emotions, motivation, and perceptions during a workday, the single most important is making progress in meaningful work.' (Amabile and Kramer, 2011)

Every time that we make progress because we've got another thing done, we get a lovely brain chemistry boost, we get dopamine hits coming that actually create more resilience in our persons and in our organisations.

The focus on 'done' also promotes a culture of experimenting which inevitably leads to innovation. So, let's look at our example before from the Australian telecommunications company, Optus. Their little experiment with the chatbot became a large-scale innovation, and it very much aligns in the world of agile to minimum viable product. The minimum viable product is a concept in Agile where you work towards doing the least amount of work to deliver something that is viable and satisfies the customers. This is where you achieve speed to market. Once in market, you then continue to deliver value via feedback and iterations.

And what I like to do with leaders is really encourage them to use that concept beyond products, think about minimum viable policies, minimum viable processes. Can we take that same concept and just make things able to be released and shared and get feedback? And that way we keep moving at speed.

Change Action #22: Consider the next change you need to deliver as a leader. What would the MVP look like?

Change Action #23: Define what you need to feel comfortable releasing a new policy, process, product or service in your business.

Shift 3: From Command and Control to Trust and Transparency

Our third shift is the move from command and control to trust and transparency. And again, I often see command and control given a bad name. We demonise people or leaders who use command and control. I think it's really important to acknowledge that command and control served us well once and it worked best in highly predictable environments. Leaders were rewarded on their ability to command and control.

So, while it is correct to identify that command and control is not the best way to lead now, it unkind to demonise leaders who use that approach. Their beliefs and attitudes will have plenty of supporting data as to why they are right. We now need to provide awareness of alternative approaches and counter evidence as to why this is a necessary mindset shift.

The interesting thing is, when you talk to employees who are operating in a command-and-control environment, they will tell you that it feels like punishment to them. Behind closed doors many leaders will tell you that it exhausts them, and they don't like that it distances them from their employees, and they don't enjoy being a command-and-control type of leader. With a bit of introspection, you may find there is ample data to support a change in belief here.

Ultimately, 'command and control' leadership styles disempower people and reduce autonomy. If we want to be effective at moving at speed in this disruptive environment, we need autonomy.

High trust and clear accountability create conditions for new ideas, new products and new services. L. David Marquet of *Turn the Ship Around* is a great resource on this. His suggestion on control is it can be tuned based on the level of competence and clarity that it provides. If your conditions are low competence and low clarity, it will be difficult to give up control. His counter leadership action is to lead by intent. Intent replaces the certainty implied in clarity and he argues for continuous building of competence about you.

Change Action #24: Start your meetings with your team by declaring the intent of what you want to do.

Change Action #25: Review the capability program with your direct reports. What learning and development needs to happen for you to loosen your grip?

Shift 4: From failure-aversion to failure-seeking

Our fourth shift is from failure-aversion to failure-seeking. Back at the Australian-Israeli Innovation Summit in 2020, a question was asked of Karin Eibschitz-Segal, Vice President, General Manager, Intel Israel Development Centre on what was the secret sauce of Israel's innovation ecosystem? Her response suggested that they are culturally rewarded to fail. Failure leads to success; it is educational and shifts perspective. Culturally, those in the innovation eco-system have courage to experiment because of the normalisation of failure-seeking.

Leaders often really struggle with this concept as they think it is a request to fail in front of the customers. They will say, 'But we can't fail in front of the customers, we will lose our customer base. We will lose revenue, and we will lose the confidence of the board.' But that is not we are talking about. The shift that leaders need to make is to how do they encourage failure-seeking within their teams, within their organisation. There are still boundaries that are prudent to be observed; failure outside the organisation is high risk.

In Amy Edmondson's HBR 2011 article Learning from Failure [2], she posits there are three types of mistakes that are made in organisations: preventable, complexity-related, and intelligent. The intelligent mistakes are the ones associated with a culture of experimentation and innovation. The preventable ones are usually the ones that leaders think they are being asked to make when the move from failure-avoidance to failure-seeking.

The leader's willingness to seek failure as part of a commitment to experimentation is directly correlated with their relationship with shame and the strength of their organisational learning process. If they believe that the failure will be a proof point that they are not worthy nor relevant, they will be most likely to engaging in blaming behaviours as a way of distancing themselves.

Equally, if the organisation does not have a strong organisational learning platform, it will be difficult to process the failure and learn from the mistakes.

So, this leads to two new change actions:

Change Action #26: Write down the last three failures that occurred under your leadership. Reflect on to what extent they damaged your brand and value. Is there evidence that they did? Or did it lead to a more innovative outcome?

Change Action #27: Investigate your organisational learning processes and platforms. Do they need to

improve to support a culture of failure seeking?

Liberation

The five topics for you to adapt your leadership styles in this chapter focus on the mindset and include:

- a more exploratory way of leading
- a beginners mindset
- a focus on execution and delivery over perfection
- releasing control and
- failure seeking

These five mindset shifts enable the navigation of fast paced disruptive change. But beyond the commercial value of thinking differently, there is a remarkable emotional energy we get out of thinking this way. It is extraordinarily liberating.

You are no longer weighed down by having to be right.

You are no longer constrained by having to be perfect.

You are no longer paralysed by not knowing all the answers.

You are no longer held back from speaking with your people because you don't have clarity.

You can let go of a mindset that no longer serves you well.

Liberation always comes at a price. The speed at which you can adopt a new mindset, a new way of thinking will depend on how much you wish to pay. It will cost you courage, bravery, and vulnerability. The next chapter, *Qualities of leaders for the future*, will help you with that.

Notes

1. https://www.itnews.com.au/news/optus-handles-84-percent-of-service-inquiries-in-its-digital-channels-557979
2. https://hbr.org/2011/04/strategies-for-learning-from-failure

Chapter 4: Qualities of leaders for the future

I suggested in the last chapter that *this* chapter would be useful in working through how you put some of the change actions of leading with an agile mindset. This chapter deals with the qualities that I have observed in leaders who lead change well.

These qualities often get relegated and dismissed as soft aspects of leadership, nice to have, if you will. My journey with developing these qualities would suggest it is quite difficult. It's not an exhaustive list by any means, but it will serve you well in navigating future disruptive change, to exhibit and indeed amplify these qualities.

Vulnerability

Vulnerability is a quality that many people feel deeply uncomfortable about and have negative associations with. And for good reason. To be vulnerable is to be putting yourself at risk of physical, emotional or psychological danger. Where the state of vulnerability can be quite confounding is that in putting yourself in that position of risk, you often find that the payoffs are high. At worst, in being openly vulnerable we open space for people to help us and support us. In Chapter One we introduced the work of researcher and author Prof Brene Brown. Brown came to light and popular acclaim through her now famous 2009 Tedx Talk the Power of Vulnerability. At best, as Brown says, vulnerability is the birthplace of innovation, creativity and change.

As a society we have been trained, socialised and brainwashed to hide vulnerability. We believe that to be vulnerable is to be weak; that people will not find us worthy of their attention or respect. We project a 'stiff upper lip' and tell people we are great when we are not. When a lot of people hit rock bottom – they lose their job, their relationship, their business or their home – they find it easier to be openly vulnerable, but only when there is nothing else to lose. It's a last resort.

But the power in vulnerability. especially in times of change, is not waiting until you hit rock bottom. The more we normalise vulnerability, so it is part of 'Business as Usual', the more likely we are to being able to access the transformative aspects of vulnerability – the innovation, the creativity and the change.

From a practical sense, if the changes that are happening with your association or organisation make you feel uncomfortable, uneasy or anxious, sharing this discomfort with your leadership team and employees can be highly beneficial. That opening up emotionally to others and being real is what creates followers and strengthens relationships. Do you recall in Chapter One where we talked about the SCARF model? The ability to be vulnerable with your colleagues and team increases 'Relatability' and reduces threat responses in change. Everyone can relate to feeling vulnerable, and the willingness to lead in a state of vulnerability lessens the distance between 'he/she/they are not like me'.

The neuroscience studies tell us that our brains are constantly making assessments on whether the person we are talking to us is 'like us' or 'not like us'. In primal terms, are you part of my tribe, or are you a threat? Letting the metaphorical cracks show gives people around you the opportunity to identify with you and relate to you. You earn the right to lead the tribe.

Armouring up, chest out, chin out and you could end up like the John Maxwell quote: *He who thinks he leads, but has no followers, is only taking a walk.*

A few years ago, I was speaking at an industry event. There was an audience of 200 change practitioners, and I had some difficult messages to deliver to them about lifting their game as a profession. They were messages that had the potential to alienate (you're not like us!). I chose to include an anecdote about fear and courage. And to share it I had to really be vulnerable (this paragraph has been deleted and reinserted several times!) The story was about how the previous year I took up pole dancing (*excellent only for core strength, not a second career*). And every week in going into that class I was the oldest by about 20 years and the heaviest by 40 kilograms. The story spoke to themes of courage and trying new things. But do you know what? That disclosure – that I'm older and heavier, and I felt really uncomfortable about it – created a relatability I could never have predicted. My messages landed with grace and ease.

A cautionary note on vulnerability. Brown will tell you there is no talk of vulnerability without consideration of boundaries. As I said at the outset, being in a position of vulnerability can place you at risk. You need to determine what your boundaries are – to what extent is it NOT prudent to be vulnerable. Oversharing can have a cost. You need to judge your team's capacity to connect first. Equally, there needs to be a genuine commitment to vulnerability. You can't 'script' vulnerability to make you seem more approachable.

Change Action #28: Note three people in your professional orbit that you could safely be a little more open with about your feelings.

Change Action #29: Review the week ahead. Where is there opportunity to be a little more vulnerable in your communication?

Empathy

In 2020 we had such a complex relationship with

empathy. Globally, we saw a tribal fracturing of society which in many cases showed a considerable empathy deficit, people just did not care about others around them when their personal pain was so great. Paradoxically, we saw incredible examples of communities coming together and offering to help neighbours who were housebound or physically vulnerable.

In the workplace, leaders were immediately expected to 'turn on empathy' for team members who had to work from home, juggle schooling and parenting responsibilities and live with family members in a much more concentrated fashion. My observation was that a lot of this empathy was one-way. There was not so much being directed at leadership teams of organisations.

Being empathic required a really conscious effort while our amygdalae were fired up in threat mode. We were also lacking the immediate physical cues of micro-expressions and mirror neurons to respond to because of the social distancing, mask-wearing and lock downs. The research shows that fatigue, stress and cognitive overload all compromise our ability to show empathy. While it would have been easy to say get better sleep, reduce stressors and reduce what's on your plate, it was much more difficult to do in the last year.

Empathy is defined as the ability to understand and share the feelings of another. Empathy does not mean agreeing with the feelings, simply understanding them and sharing what it means to feel those emotions. Daniel Goleman, the pioneer in the space of emotional intelligence, has classified three types of empathy.

1) Cognitive empathy – a mental sense of how another's thinking works. How do we best communicate with another? We don't connect on an emotional level, but we can understand how the other is thinking.

2) Emotional empathy – this means we pick up on others facial, vocal, and non-verbal signals and permits the acceleration of rapport though the building of trust.

3) Empathetic concern – how do we support and care for another?

Empathetic concern moves beyond the intellectual and emotional recognition and validation to action; what are we going to do about the situation that is being expressed? This third challenge – what are we going to do – is the genesis of many great change designs, and not surprisingly you will find that empathy is a core component of designing good change experiences. All design thinking approaches have empathy for customer or employee as one of the fundamental steps in the process. As you start to design what your organisation of the future looks like you will need to tap into a broader empathy for how society has changed because of the pandemic.

When you can seek to understand another person's view, you can design the change experience, so it is better for them (and offers less resistance). If you can really empathise, this helps your decision-making as you understand the potential consequences of it.

Empathy also becomes a conduit to better communication and collaboration. When we feel that the other person understands us and validates us, it builds trust. We forgive misunderstandings more easily and are more prepared to share mutual outcomes. But beyond the utility in change, empathy is key to working through trauma, and 2020 will have created a traumatised workforce. Empathy is also important to change leadership during disruption as it creates an environment where it is safe to fail. It encourages leaders to understand the root cause behind failures.

I noted before that I thought empathy had been remarkably one-way during the last year – who was showing empathy for the leaders? Change leadership is undeniably a tough gig and it's not often one that is publicly acknowledged as such. This is where your relationship with vulnerability will pay off. If you are more comfortable with being open about being in a struggle, you may find that your peers or team will come forward from a place of empathy.

Change Action #30: End of week huddle: ask everyone to share a professional high and low and focus on responding with empathy.

Change Action #31: Go out for a coffee by yourself and spend time watching people and trying to imagine what is going on in their world.

Curiosity

Curiosity is the great enabler of change and transformation. It offers us tools to find better ways, quicker paths, easier efforts.

- I wonder?
- What change is needed?
- What is the vision for the future?
- What should not be altered?
- What behaviours need to be changed? Modified? Kept the same?
- What performance indicators will show success?
- How could we?
- Why might we?

By consciously embracing a curious mindset to the work in front of you, you move into exploration of how to do things better and easier. This is why curiosity is such an important aspect of the Exploratory Leader referred to in the previous chapter.

The curious mind seeks out new platforms, new skill

sets, new opportunities. It acts as a circuit breaker to premature judgment. Leaders who foster curiosity enable a shift in view, one that can be more empathic and therefore design change intentionally and more successfully. Curiosity can be a challenging quality to adopt when leading change or being an agent of change, primarily because it takes time. You need to sit with curiosity and let ideas 'marinate'. It is very time efficient to know things and be sure of things. Our organisations reward that. As such, it needs a commitment from leaders to nurture a culture that supports the inefficiencies of curiosity.

Some of the reasons why we want to cultivate curiosity is that it will build a growth mindset and thus build a resilience that is useful in a relentlessly changing world. Curiosity is also a quality that overcomes the defensiveness associated with resistance to change, and it is the openness it creates that is necessary for innovation and change.

Erik Shonstrom's book *Wild Curiosity* is also a really good read on the topic. In it, he introduces us to Jordan Litman's research on curiosity. Litman proposes a more nuanced view of curiosity, and two categories.

- **D-type curiosity**, which suggests that our curiosity is piqued by having a deficit in some way. Our drive is therefore to learn something that's important to us.

- **I-type curiosity** is more curiosity for the sake of curiosity.

It's rather like the pain and pleasure motivation states. We get curious when we are in pain and need to solve a problem and we get curious when we get joy and pleasure out of new ideas. And to that end they can be considered motivations at either end of a spectrum.

If you think of it that way, a lot of our product innovation comes from D-type motivations, but when we start to play with things like 'hack days' and 'what if / how could we?' sessions, we are tapping into 'I-type' curiosity. I suspect that you will find that your change of the future comes from more activity in I-type curiosity. The intentionality of D-type curiosity can take us down paths that are familiar to us already, we seek our information that confirms what we think. There is novelty in I-type curiosity.

It is highly likely, though, that we haven't given it much conscious thought at all. For so long curiosity has been the domain of creatives, philosophers, artists, inventors and scientists.

It's only recently that we have seen fit to add curiosity to job descriptions of people in business. And that's because we now know that curiosity primes the brain for retention of knowledge. There's a strong correlation between people who are naturally curious and people who know a lot!

It is highly likely that 2020 saw a reduction in your levels of curiosity. We know that when we are distracted with being busy and fatigued, we also lack curiosity. The bombardment of conflicting information from organisations, governments and social media meant that our ability to listen carefully was diminished. Listening is the medium for identifying cues, red and green flags of things to be curious about. Let this part of the book serve as an alert – it is time to actively amp up your curiosity again.

It can also raise the question, what are other barriers to curiosity? Einstein had something to say on that:

> It is nothing short of a miracle that modern methods of instruction have not yet entirely strangled the holy curiosity of inquiry. For this delicate little plant, aside from stimulation, stands mainly in need of freedom.

And freedom is often in short supply in our organisations. If we think back to Chapter One and the discussion on power, most organisations operate with *power over* as the dominant model of governance (command and control). It is only when we move to the *power with* and *shared power* models that we create freedom for curiosity to grow. If you want to build curiosity in your organisation, you need to build safety and freedom.

Change Action #32: Notice when you move to judgment and the time it takes to do so.

Change Action #33: Create 30 minutes in your week to explore something without an agenda.

Change Action #34: Seek surprise – ask one of your employees or colleagues to tell you something you don't know that you should know.

Courage

Often when we think about bravery and courage we think about big acts of courage. Leaving the abusive partner, running into a burning house to save a child, leaving a well-paid job of 20 years to do something new and high risk. It requires extraordinary energy. And people marvel afterwards – 'Oh you were brave!'

But the quality that leaders will need to build in abundance is perhaps better thought about as micro-moments of courage. Small acts of courage. The courage to be decisive knowing that some people you respect will not be happy with you as it means for a period they will be in a position of loss. Juggling the various positions on the change you are leading is exhausting. And while you remain in a state of consensus or collective decision-making you continually have balls in the air and are in a semi-state of paralysis. You need courage to take a course of action, if it's only a small step forward.

Adopting a *power with* approach to leadership will require courage – the redistribution of power and control. If you are used to controlling everything, then empowering others is quite courageous.

It will be courageous to reprioritise and put some of the things your organisation does on hold, to abandon previous agendas and focus on what needs to be done. It can also be considered brave to say 'No' to your leadership team, or your board, to hold out for empathy and safety when it is more expedient to cut costs.

It is courageous to acknowledge as leader of change that you have too much on your plate, to prioritise self-care and mental health. Like vulnerability, *bravery as BAU* will pay off.

Many of you will be familiar with the metaphor of the burning platform shared by Daryl Conner in his book the *Managing at the Speed of Change*. Many of you might think you need to create a fire before you can get people to change. It turns out that's not what the metaphor is about. It's about courage and commitment.

In 1988 Conner was watching a news story of the Alpha Piper oil rig disaster in the North Sea off the coast of Scotland, where 166 crew members and two rescuers lost their lives. One of the surviving crew members was Andy Mochan, a superintendent on the rig. On the news show he described the courage and commitment it required to jump off the platform which would mean facing probable death. The freezing water was littered with burning oil and steel shards. At that temperature he had only 20 minutes in the water to stay alive. Staying on the platform meant certain death. And in that moment, watching the show, Conner recognised that same mindset and behaviour in what he was seeing in business leaders who were being successful in change. Courage and commitment.

What we know from behavioural change research, though, is if you focus on making bravery BAU, and identify, enact and reward small acts of courage on a regular basis, you don't need as much energy to be brave. It doesn't have to be a leap from a burning platform.

I think one of the reasons why courage will be such an important leadership attribute for times of continuing disruption is that organisationally, economically, societally and politically, we default to decisions and policies based on fear. Making decisions based on fear is not necessarily bad, it can be prudent and lifesaving. However, if all decisions are made based on fear than we can expect a very constrained world, and one that spirals inwards and downwards. There will be no innovation, no new frontiers. It will be Groundhog Day until such time as our resources are expired. It's kind of bleak, right?

As Nelson Mandela said, '*Courage is not the absence of fear, but the triumph over it.*'

Change Action #35: Identify one domain where you could be 10% braver and take action.

Change Action #36: Reflect on who demonstrates courage in your immediate circles. Is it bravery as usual or a leaping from a burning platform kind of courage?

(Mindful) Self-compassion

The final quality you will need to cultivate is perhaps the most difficult. It is the bedrock of the previous four: self-compassion. Many leaders struggle with this as it is contrasted by the state of judgment. And all leaders have been rewarded, lauded and promoted on their ability to make good judgments. Judging is what you do! The ability to switch off a state of judgment is difficult to acquire when it is the source of your leadership power.

Judgment sits in the way of compassion for self and compassion for others. When you sit in judgment, it is difficult to access empathy. You most definitely cannot do curiosity. Judgment makes sure vulnerability doesn't get a look in, and judgment makes the energy needs for courage extraordinary. When you build your ability to apply self-compassion all those qualities become easier.

In my conversations with leaders, time after time, this is the element that they baulk at. I routinely ask guests on my podcast what their relationship is with self-compassion and it is the answer that is the most wordy, unwieldly and disjointed. And yet the research [1] is clear: those leaders with a self-compassion practice have higher emotional intelligence, are more resilient and create organisations with greater psychological safety. These three elements lead to increased innovation and higher performance.

The standard self-compassion question is 'Would you treat your best friend the way you treat yourself?', and you can substitute best friend with any loved one, but inevitably the contrast is significantly strong. We don't give ourselves as much grace, as much acceptance, as much love as we do others in our life.

Self-compassion researcher and expert, Kristin Neff tells us that self-compassion has three elements:

1) Self-kindness
2) Common Humanity
3) Mindfulness

Self-kindness is contrasted with the predisposition to judge oneself and be our worst critic. It describes our ability to be gentle with ourselves in the face of failure and imperfection. You can see the tie in with agile mindsets shifts. When we move from a mindset of perfection and failure aversion, we are also taking a kinder approach to leading organisations through change and disruption.

Common Humanity draws our attention to the fact that the frustration we feel at things not being perfect is simple part of what it means to be human. While it often feels like you are the only one making mistakes, embodying a self-compassionate view means you recognise you are not alone, that many make the same mistakes.

Mindfulness requires that we step into an observant phase of our feelings. We cannot have compassion for self if we are denying the discomfort of pain. By taking a more mindful approach to our emotions we neither exaggerate what is going on or diminish it. We simply acknowledge the emotions we feel.

In her work with Christopher Germer, Neff distinguishes mindfulness as focusing on the acceptance of the **experience**, while self-compassion is focused on the acceptance of the **experiencer**.

This makes sense to me because increasingly in organisational life we see 'medicinal mindfulness' play out. Medicinal mindfulness is what I call the approach we take to stress – we schedule yoga, set alarms to do Calm / Mindspace / Insight Timer spot meditations – but the stress does not abate in any substantive way.

We are using mindfulness to soldier on through, but by ignoring the self-compassion aspect, we don't really change anything. We are still just 'white knuckling' through. It is only when you combine self-compassion with mindfulness that you start to change the full experience of leading through continuing disruption.

Change Action #37: Draft a supportive and encouraging note to yourself on how you are handling the current challenges. Write it as if you were writing to your best friend.

Change Action #38: Download Insight Timer app on your phone and find a loving kindness meditation to listen to.

This chapter has introduced you to the importance of:

- Empathy
- Vulnerability
- Courage
- Curiosity
- and Mindful Self-Compassion.

Its not unusual to feel a little tender when considering these topics – and so my strongest advice when making changes in this direction is to go slow and go with support. The more these qualities are integrated and lived in your day-to-day life the less they are challenging for you.

Continue to ask yourself, what can I do to be 5% more courageous, curious, empathetic, vulnerable and self-compassionate? This continued introspection will make you so much more strong, so much more resilient, so much more flexible. Which is a good thing – you're going to need that for leading in continued uncertainty, something the next chapter picks up on.

Notes

1. https://hbr.org/2020/11/self-compassion-will-make-you-a-better-leader

Chapter 5: Leading through uncertainty

I noted earlier in Chapter One my bemusement with how earnestly we have used the descriptor volatile, uncertain, complex, and ambiguous (VUCA) to describe our operating environment. In networking events, breakfasts, lunches, dinners and conferences on the topic of business agility, executives earnestly nod their heads in acknowledgement that they are operating in a VUCA environment.

And while I could always agree with them about the *uncertainty* and *complexity* aspects, I often challenged the *volatility* and the *ambiguity*. Because I didn't think that many organisations really operated in volatile and ambiguous environments. Fast-moving – yes, multiple parts moving within paradoxes – also yes, but not volatile or ambiguous.

The spread of COVID-19 and accompanying

economic downturn and widespread corporate and government work-from-home resulted in truly volatile conditions. We saw information and news changing hour-to-hour, bringing with them multiple interpretations of policies and Business Continuity Plans. It showed that most leaders and senior managers were unprepared for a truly volatile, uncertain, complex and ambiguous environment.

Inarguably, leading through uncertainty was one of the greatest tests put to leaders in 2020. And while this is a challenge that has always existed, somehow the uncertainty, in 2020 was, I don't know... even MORE uncertain! And it continues to be. Part of this was a natural predisposition to expect that things would return to normal. In the face of continuing NOT returning to normal, not only did leaders face challenges on leading through uncertainty but also the additional load of cognitive dissonance. The internal monologue went something like 'I believe it to be true that we will return to normal, but it is not yet, and I don't understand why!'

The ability to lead through uncertainty is predicated on multiple factors. These factors include the ability to use data well, use strategic foresight tools, and embody calm in yourself and in others. Success is founded as much on the technical tools and skills needed to make sense of data and anticipate new scenarios, but also the mental, physical and emotional abilities to exist in a state of equanimity.

Equanimity is a state of stability and composure

which is undisturbed by experience of or exposure to emotions, pain or extreme variations in life. You can float with the variability, neither in denial, in exultation nor in catastrophe.

Cultivating a state of equanimity is a calculated and considered effort. If you recall in Chapter One, our brains privilege certainty, and when faced with a lack of certainty, react in survival mode (shallow breathing, conserving food / water, high speed emotional responses, diminished cognitive capacity). We react instinctively to a lack of certainty.

Data informed decision making

Let's look first at the technical tools and skills. One of the biggest areas to build your capability in is data informed decision-making. When you know that you will naturally respond emotionally and in survival mode, you need to supplement that response with a clear data informed position.

In organisational life, we have access to strategic data and operational data. Stewart Bird, Digital Futures Leader of global engineering firm Aurecon describes this as data we can *exploit* and data we can *explore* [1].

Data we can exploit refers to data that drives efficiency in the business – so for example, automation of processes, and the data that is codifying, digitising and productising knowledge from the organisation. With this data we can reduce the repetitive manual tasks in the organisation. In an ideal world this creates a positive redundancy and what is known as organisational slack. It's the freeing up of people from things that were once repetitive, that they had to do again, and again, and again.

Liberation from repetition means creating space to learn new things and innovate on what they do in order to create new value. In Chapter Four I said that one of the barriers to curiosity is not having time – slack is how you enable curiosity in the workforce. When you engineer slack out of the system you engineer the innovation out of the system. You cannot engage in 'I-type' curiosity without time to explore, and this in our organisational life relates to slack.

Data we can explore is the type of data that provides signals of change around and within the organisation. Bird explains:

'It could be looking at the financial markets. Where is money being redistributed to? Is that telling us something about changing consumption patents or investment patents? Is that telling us something about changes in the wider economic landscape? Or it could be more sort of information artifacts. It could be news articles. It could be blog posts, journal articles, researching or exploring topics, and that is where we're seeing that there's interest, potential signals that something might be changing. There are developments in different technologies.

'And by using that data, we can start to identify where there might be trends that might be growing. Might be just early weak signals of change. And from there, we can do the implications and scenario analysis. If that were to take off, if that were to accelerate, what would that mean for our business? What would that mean for our clients' businesses? What would that mean for our end-users, or customers, or the communities that we live in? What do these things mean and what sort of actions do we really need to take today to make sure that we are not exposed to risks that might be thrown up? Or we are really positioning ourselves for opportunities that that is going to present to us, that change'.

Building a proficiency and maturity in sourcing, curating and processing data, both operational and strategic, will be core to how you lead through continuing disruption. Not every organisation has a mature data ecosystem, so at the simplest level, you can start by making sure that all your change efforts are informed by a discussion on what the data tells you, whether it be financial data, consumer insights or data from Human Resources.

You manage risk by having these discussions on a frequent basis, understanding the volatility of data available to you, and adapting your efforts based on subsequent data delivered. Leading through uncertainty is leading through paradox and one of the tensions you need to hold is that of pivot or persevere.

If you are relying on highly volatile data to inform your decision-making, your challenge will be: at what point do I change direction and at what point do I hold? It is here that the explorer's mindset noted in Chapter Three and the qualities in Chapter Four of curiosity, courage, vulnerability, and self-compassion come into play to support you.

Change Action #39: Review the extent to which you are using data in your decision- making. Is it operational data to exploit efficiency? Is it strategic to explore opportunities?

Change Action #40: Catalogue the sources of data you currently use in your decision- making. Where are there gaps?

Uncertainty Reduction

Much of what we know about reducing uncertainty comes from the domain of information and communication theory and so these flows into the leadership communication that you do. Many of my clients in leadership positions prefer not communicating until they have certainty, but this is more about the mindsets discussed in Chapter Three that represent failure aversion and perfectionism.

Best practice uncertainty reduction is to provide small slices of information on a frequent and regular basis. As we learnt in the last chapter, demonstrating some vulnerability can have payoffs and support your communication through uncertainty. This might look like 'At the moment, I / we don't have all of the answers as to what lies ahead, but what I can commit to you is to provide frequent regular updates.'

You do have opportunities to embed 'anchors of stability'. When your employees are hyper-alert to things that are changing, you can stack your communications with what is staying the same. These messages of stability will need to be repeated to take purchase. Being deliberate and intentional on how to communicate what is enduring, not changing, and can be relied on, can have strong calming effects.

The other area to build up in your leadership communication to promote uncertainty reduction is sense-making. Consciously creating opportunities for people to discuss what is happening and advance theories or potential scenarios helps people make sense of what they do not understand. Because our brains privilege certainty we will already be trying to connect the dots, but in the absence of your input that dot connection can go askew. It is better to shape the opportunities for sense-making in your organisation, than let people's independent sense-making dominate with incorrect information.

Future-casting and strategic foresight

One of the ways to supplement information and assist in sense-making is to take a transparent future-casting approach (often known as strategic foresight). Traditionally, future-casting occurs in the domain of strategy, but if you are moving towards a model of 'power with' and seeking to diversify the thinking in your organisation, then this can be a useful approach to take with teams that go beyond the strategy team.

Future casting [2] involves using tools to look at the

exploratory data and signals in your environment and to generate potential scenarios and analyse the probabilities. At an individual level, the question 'what if' is known to generate significant anxiety and a simple remedy for this is to write down the answers to your 'what if' questions. This is an organisational version of the same process.

Bird explains:

'A lot of people will think it's sort of crystal ball type stuff, or sci-fi storytelling. But what we're really trying to do is to understand complex systems. We want to understand how systems interact with one another. We want to know if there was a change in one of those systems, how that is going to cascade through a whole range of other systems that it interacts with. And, of course, in today's world, we're far more interconnected than ever before. We live in complex environments. We operate in complex environments where changes in one part of the world will cascade or have the potential to really cascade throughout all facets of our economies and our work.

'So, what we're trying to do is to look at where those changes are likely to occur and what those flow-on effects are going to be. And then, work with stakeholders around the business, leaders around the business to design actions, design initiatives, design projects that are going to put us in a good position should those things start to affect our business. Allow us to profit from them, more in anticipation rather than being super reactive to them.'

Change Action #41: Review your leadership communications for the week ahead. What are the stability messages in them?

Change Action #42: Review your leadership communications for the quarter ahead. How can you increase the frequency and 'slice' the information further? What are the opportunities for sense-making?

Keep calm

Data informed decision-making, future casting and uncertainty reduction have a strong emphasis on technical tools. The ability to drive a state of equanimity and keep calm relies on tools or tactics that are not so technical in nature.

In essence, what we are doing is seeking to reduce the threat to survival in our brain that is triggered with continuous change. The ability to keep calm is highly contagious, it has a viral effect on others, especially if you are in position of power.

When leading, how do we help people to calm?

Ground yourself first

The metaphor is somewhat overused, but nonetheless appropriate. In the safety briefing on airplanes, we are told that if travelling with an infant or child, give oxygen to ourselves first before giving to the younger one. The principle stays the same here.

You need to find a way to *ground* yourself so that you are calm.

Grounding yourself is finding a way to balance your emotional, mental and physical states so you consciously manage your energy. Grounding techniques are similar to the those we see in the 'mindfulness' movement.

There are dozens of grounding techniques available to you and they range from the hardcore metaphysical 'woo' of covering the crown of your head and sinking feet into the earth and standing like a tree, to the basic physiological breathing, immersing in cold water, and inhaling the scent of your morning coffee. It is your choice what you do, but absolutely not negotiable that you do it.

Change Action #43: Identify a grounding technique that works for you and practice daily.

Address the chemistry of stress

Once you are grounded you will be attentive to the neurobiology and chemistry of stress. In Chapter One we talked how the brain reacts to change and the threat triggers. What we didn't talk about is how when the amygdala or limbic system is inflamed and firing off a 'fight, flight, freeze' response, it also pumps out stress hormones, namely adrenalin which increases heart rate and elevates blood pressure (to help you fight or flee), and cortisol which increases sugars in your body (again to repair tissues in fight or flight) and reduces the non-essential functions in your body, so your body purely is focused on keeping you alive.

An example of a non-essential function in a crisis is digestion; therefore, when people are stressed, they have digestive function difficulties or put on weight. Metabolic processing is non-essential. Adrenalin and cortisol are valuable in an emergency, but once your brain thinks it is an emergency continuously, the surplus supplies of these stress hormones is detrimental to our health and sleep patterns.

Activating good hormones like dopamine, serotonin, and oxytocin is an effective way to counter the stress hormones. Some of the methods of increasing these 'happiness hormones' are to encourage laughter, show appreciation, be social, exercise and access sunlight.

Change Action #44: At the end of each week, write five 'thank-you' notes and send to people in your organisation.

Open heart and open mind

We do not tend to talk about love and heart-based practice in the workplace all that much. But the act of giving and receiving love is calming. It makes you feel good to **be compassionate** and it makes others feel reassured to receive compassion. There is an active debate over the concept of compassion / empathy fatigue. One set of researchers will tell you that compassion bolsters feel good hormones, empathy activates the stress hormones as it is experienced as shared pain. The other camp tells you the opposite, that compassion is a subset of empathy and empathy activates the feel-good hormones.

The pragmatic reality is that only a small percentage of the population (notably carers, social workers and nurses) are likely to experience compassion or empathy fatigue. Most of the population and indeed the leadership population underplay compassion and empathy. The debate is a distraction from being a leader who instils calm through showing compassion and an open mind. You can demonstrate an open mind by listening attentively to people. This makes people feel valued, but also opens the possibility that other people may have some clever ideas.

Change Action #45: Clear space in your diary to have a session with a direct report with no agenda, just to listen to their thoughts.

Reinforce stability

If your brain is a state of high alert and threat to survival, to some extent you need to trick it into recognising that things are still 'normal', and you are safe. This means reinforcing the mundane, the repeated and the usual. Earlier we spoke of including stability messages in your leadership communication, but this also extends to your organisational routines. Many leaders in 2020 increased their check-ins with team members as they were working from home.

Some of this activity was out of care and compassion, some of it was a form of additional surveillance because they were no longer within eyesight. For many, the increased check-ins were stressful. Autonomy was challenged. As you navigate the continuing disruptions there is opportunity to pause and reflect on what is a 'normal' cadence of contact with your people. Perhaps do this reflection with your people to understand what feels best for them. Work with your teams to determine which old rituals you wish to reinforce and what are new rituals to anchor and create stability.

Change Action #46: Identify three things that have stayed the same over the last 18 months.

You only have one body, treat it well.

In Chapter Four, we spoke of the importance of self-compassion. Looking after yourself physically is an act of self-care and self-compassion. To embody calm you need to be hydrated and breathing well. Sometimes this needs to be a conscious activity.

- Set your alarms on your watch or phone.
- Give yourself reminders.
- Invite others to drink water and breathe well.

If you have ever done a hot yoga class you will know that they emphasise above all else, stay in the room. This is because the act of inhaling heated air can induce the sympathetic nervous system and triggers flight response.

If you are dehydrated and shallow breathing, you will be inducing panic in your body. The same applies to the people you lead, a gentle reminder to breathe and stay hydrated will create much reprieve.

Change Action #47: Stop and take seven breaths.

Change Action #48: Stop and drink a glass of water.

This chapter has suggested that when leading through uncertainty you be attentive to four topics:

- data informed decision making
- uncertainty reduction
- strategic forecasting
- and keeping calm.

Focusing on these four aspects of our current conditions may accelerate your ability to be opportunistic with change, rather than responding to forced change. Despite this optimistic frame there will still be challenges, and we will pick these up in the next chapter: Obstacles you will face.

Notes

1. https://drjenfrahm.com/leading-change-with-data/
2. https://hbr.org/2019/07/how-to-do-strategic-planning-like-a-futurist

Chapter 6: The obstacles you will face

Now in applying all the 48 change actions offered so far, it's fair to say that you will still be facing considerable challenges in leading through continued disruptive change. In the spirit of preparing, you well, let's look at five of the most common obstacles to leading change.

You will not feel safe

You will continue to be feeling a sense of heightened risk and lack of safety for several reasons:

Your peers may not have the same commitment to leading change that you do and may be reverting to poor behaviours on account of stress. This leads you to feel like you are in hand-to-hand combat within your own leadership team. In Chapter One, I noted the importance of creating psychologically safe environments. In the years since Amy Edmondson's 2014 TEDx on the concept of psychological safety has become popular, most of our application is in considering psychological safety for the employees.

Very rarely to do we recognise that leaders exist within a system where there may be retribution for taking interpersonal risks, such as speaking up and challenging status quo. We know that psychological safety is connected to a whole stack of good things – creativity, learning, innovation, trust constructive conflict and engagement, but on the shadow side, the lack of psychological safety at a leadership level is rarely discussed.

The challenge with a lack of safety is if the leader is not feeling safe, he or she will be experiencing heightened arousal of the amygdala and limbic system. We know from our basic studies of neuroscience that when our amygdala is 'hijacked' (to use Daniel Goleman's term), it is less likely that we will be in high performance mode cognitively. We will do more stupid things.

If we are doing more stupid things, it is likely that we will be scrutinised and ridiculed by peers and media. You don't have to look far to see you are now operating in an environment of trial by social media. The additional layers of scrutiny and transparency means you are open to criticism by many more than your leadership peers. The potential of press or peer shaming can act as a significant deterrent to leading change.

A lack of safety can also be identified by the leader's noting they have been handed a poisoned chalice – something that initially looks like a great opportunity, but ultimately will bring about the downfall of the benefactor. In more modern times than Macbeth's, and impacting women considerably more than men, this has come to be identified as a glass cliff. While glass ceilings are invisible barrier to promotion for women, glass cliffs are precarious positions of leadership from which they can fall.

The term was coined in 2004 by British professors Michelle K. Ryan and Alexander Haslam of the University of Exeter in the UK. Ryan and Haslam examined the performance of FTSE 100 companies before and after the appointment of new board members, and found that companies that appointed women to their boards were more likely than others to have experienced consistently bad performance in the preceding five months .

Women are more likely to be appointed to senior leadership roles during organisational crisis (and therefore less likely to succeed). The under-representation of women in executive roles means that when offered a prime executive role, a woman is less likely to be attentive to the danger in front of her, as the risk / reward assessment is skewed. Since the term originated, its use has expanded beyond the corporate world to also encompass politics and other domains.

When the leader realises that the opportunity of a lifetime is ultimately something that has been doomed to fail and they have been put in as a fall guy or gal, they have both a sense of disappointment and betrayal. You may find that survival mode kicks in and it is safer to stay out of the limelight until a safer, more certain change comes through. In these circumstances, only the most courageous and committed of leaders will continue to lead change through disruption.

As noted in Chapter Four on qualities, courage ultimately defines most leaders of change. Like the story of the 'Burning Platform' and Andy Mochan in Chapter Four, the superintendent who leapt from a burning platform despite the freezing water littered with shards and flames, leadership of change represents certain danger, glass cliffs or not, and requires commitment and courage to see it through.

Change Action #49: Identify your safety net. Pause and do a 360-degree review; what are the elements and who are the people who make you feel safer?

You won't like your peers

It is not uncommon to see a leadership team in conflict in times of struggle.

History is full of examples where the leadership team members do not like each other. It's hard to stay focused on your people and leading change if you are concerned that you will be sabotaged or white-anted by your peers or are holding feelings of antipathy for them.

A mistrust or dislike of the leadership team members is often derived from two main areas – recognising a lack of capability in the executive team (he or she is not up to the job) or recognising that your peers have a different motivation to yours.

Make no mistake, conflict in the senior leadership team will create unnecessary delays in decision-making, risk aversion and the creation of organisational silos, all factors that are detrimental to leading through disruptive change.

Some of the ways to improve this situation have already been highlighted in this book so far and represent a set of change actions:

- Review the situation in front of you or the team member you do not rate through the lens of compassion and curiosity. What might be going on for them that is causing them to behave the way they are? It may be that the past executive hiring strategy has prioritised talents and experience better suited to less disruptive times.

- Consider what their strengths are and what they bring to the table; have you and your peers neglected to recognise strengths that have been overshadowed by the Covid-19 pandemic? As covered in Chapter One, our go-to strengths in our Business-as-Usual mode may be vastly different in disruptive change. It's probably fairer to have an explicit leadership conversation about what strengths need to be marshalled now.

- Take the emotional heat out of the situation by turning to data informed decision- making – it's not personal, it's the data that tells you the way forward.

- Acknowledge the friction brought forward by thought diversity. It's normal to do things differently to your peers. Diverse teams outperform homogenous teams considerably. The problem is that by the end of 2020 you would have been in a sustained threat mode for longer than any other time in your career. This means it's possible that you will be viewing actions through the lens of 'Is this person one of my tribe or are they a threat?' And once on high alert for threats, you will be creating a bias that is difficult to challenge. So, revisit the section on activating the feel-good hormones of dopamine, adrenalin, oxytocin and serotine and reduce the cognitive filter that skews your perception of your peers.

- Review your strategies for the Axis of Collaboration and how your deal with low trust scenarios.

- Re-run the Braving Inventory – people who live in glass houses should not throw stones. Make space for the possibility that you are the source of the conflict and some of your shadow behaviours are showing up on a regular basis.

Change Action #50: Conduct a strength spotting conversation with someone you don't think highly of.

Imposter syndrome

Again, this was discussed in Chapter One on the topic of shame. The year 2020 will have left many normally confident and self-assured leaders with a sharp case of imposter syndrome.

Imposter Syndrome is defined as 'a collection of feelings of inadequacy that persist despite evident success.' 'Imposters' suffer from chronic self-doubt and a sense of intellectual fraudulence that overrides any feelings of success or external proof of their competence. [1]

It leads to procrastinating, slowing down to make things perfect, taking too much time to prepare and not speaking your mind when it counts. These impacts cost you in agility and responsiveness.

Because there is no precedent for leading through a pandemic or climate crisis, many will for the first time doubt their ability to do so. It's not like MBA courses were running simulations on how to lead through this past year (strategic foresight units excluded).

Many leaders have had to white-knuckle, best guess,

and stumble their way through the last year (and are continuing to do so). There has been no opportunity to perfect conversations, speeches, presentations or thinking. And so, feelings of shame will rise – '*I am not worthy, I am not relevant*'. As noted in Chapter One, those feelings of shame paralyse or push others away.

Valerie Young, Ed.D. an internationally recognised expert on impostor syndrome and author of the award-winning book *The Secret Thoughts of Successful Women: Why Capable People Suffer from Impostor Syndrome and How to Thrive in Spite of It*, makes some very insightful observations in her 2017 TED Talk 'Thinking your way out of Imposter Syndrome'.

She notes that the feelings of being an imposter are the last to change. If you can change your thoughts through reframing and recognise that people without imposter syndrome simply think differently, you can reduce the paralysis that goes along with feeling like an imposter. The body cannot tell the difference between fear and excitement, so you might as well just tell yourself that you're excited. The ability to recognise when feelings of doubt are normal are also important – it's valid to feel like you are unprepared when facing things for the first time.

The lack of occupational diversity will have contributed to newfound feelings of imposter syndrome and be impeding the ability to lead change through further disruption. The Robert Half CEO tracker research tells us that 50% of the CEOs in the ASX200 have a background in finance.

Many leaders come from accounting, economics and science. These occupations are not known for extraverted behaviours like thinking out loud or improvisation. They are increasingly detailed occupations dependent on being right and correct, not rewarded for risk taking, or speaking publicly. Until diversity and inclusion initiatives include occupational diversity in leadership, leaders who are currently feeling like they are an imposter, or not good enough, will be wise to try the following change action:

Change Action #51: Have a conversation with yourself from the perspective of your best friend. What would they advise you on your feelings of unworthiness?

You will still want to control

Variations of 'Command and Control' have been the dominant models of leadership and governance for thousands of years. Certainly, since the inception of modern leadership theory, most organisations have been built on Taylorist notions of efficiency, a chain of command, and spans of control. Contemporary leadership and modern organisations eschew command and control, and indeed often demonise it.

I think this is a little unfair and does not recognise that Command and Control and Taylorism served a purpose that was contextually sound. It made sense in very predictable environments. Where it has become problematic is that the context has changed (way before 2020) and many leaders have been slow to recognise this and adapt how they think about governance. The speed with which one is reluctant to give up the belief that they can control change is predicated on some of the factors we have discussed so far such as shame and vulnerability but also safety and competence.

If you do not feel safe, you will hold on to control for as long as you can. The excruciating vulnerability that goes along with the sense of free-falling is too much.

Equally, if you do not trust the competence of others, then it is unlikely you will be keen on handing over control. The prospect of things going wrong on your watch will bring about intense feelings of shame.

But here is the thing. Your environment is now way too complex and ambiguous to maintain singular control as a leader. This is why I started the book with introducing the concept of power over – power with. The desire to maintain control is an example of power over. And rather than makes things safer, it amplifies risk, it becomes a form of key man risk (where risk is concentrated in one person).

L.David Marquet, author of *Turn the Ship Around*, is a great resource on this. He suggests control can be reduced based on the level of competence and clarity that's provided. If your working environment includes low competence and low clarity, it will be difficult to give up control. His counter leadership action is to lead by intent. Intent replaces the certainty implied in clarity and he argues for continuous building of competence in those around you.

So, for example, you provide the intent of the task or strategy to deploy, and you give control to those who are closest to the ability to execute. If the competence is sufficient and the intent is understood, the leader does not need to take control. It goes without saying, this is very much in the spirit of 'power with' rather than 'power over'.

Some of the following change actions come from Marquet's book.

Change Action #52: Use 'I intend to…' to turn passive followers into active leaders.

Change Action #53: Resist the urge to provide solutions – sit in the uncertainty a little longer.

Change Action #54: Specify goals, not methods.

You will want to be liked

In traditional leadership theory, we paid a lot of attention to the psychology of leadership. There were three constructs that were important to leadership needs according to noted psychologist David McClelland. These were a need for affiliation (or social bonding, people to like us), need for achievement, and a need for power.

Traditionally, good leaders tended to score high on need for achievement and power, and low on need for affiliation. In more recent research, there's evidence that need for achievement weighs more heavily in the success of leaders in agile environments, but the findings have shifted somewhat on transformational leaders. Within this population, it seems that having a high need for affiliation engenders more followership and it's positive. But if over-played, it becomes problematic, known as an 'over-played strength'.

As noted in Chapter One, within the positive psychology movement we have seen the rolling out of strength-based leadership and the move towards motivating people based on their strengths, with a corresponding benefit of people flourishing at work. We don't see as much attention apportioned to over-played strengths. An over-played strength is one where in deploying your strength too much you get an opposite and contradictory effect.

So, leaders who have a high need to be liked exhibit more pro-social behaviour (caring, engagement, support), but in their quest to be liked, step back from activities which may be unpopular, or cause people not to like them (e.g., announcing a change or explaining how the decision was made). A very high need to be liked can be associated with an accompanying shame trigger, 'They won't like me', and it compromises your ability to make tough decisions.

This fear of not being liked is often greater for the leader than the likelihood of it the workforce not actually liking the leader. In the research in organisational change, the work done on 'procedural justice' tells us that if the change is perceived to be fair and just, the people on the other end of the decision-making accept it well.

A high need for affiliation also might indicate a person who is conflict avoidant. Think back to the last time you conflicted with someone. Did you like them much at that point? No, didn't think so.

Being the front public vocal face of change means that you are the front public vocal face of conflict. Your people may express concern and dissent, outrage, and a sense of betrayal. A desire to be liked will get in the way of navigating conversations of conflict. However, the research on this is so strong. Conflict can be a source of coming up with better ideas. By engaging with conflict, you create opportunities for stronger followership. It's easier to be respected.

Change Action #55: Question your reluctance to act. To what extent is it based on a need for people to like you?

You do not like The Messy

Change and transformation can be very, very messy. Throw in all the external environmental changes happening now and the messiness of normal change is amplified by an extraordinary amount. By nature, change is complex work that we do, high on uncertainty, and usually rich in ambiguity. And not everyone relishes that space. You have to lead with things happening that you cannot quantify, things happening that you can't categorise, things happening that you can't organise. As noted in the earlier section on diversity, many leaders have come from backgrounds who do everything possible to tidy up the messy. Quantify. Categorise. Organise. Wrap it up in a ribbon and put it on a shelf.

A fear of The Messy is often born of one of two conditions – anxiety and / or perfectionism.

When we look at anxiety in leadership, we need to decide if the anxiety is a disabling form of low mental health, or if it is a more generic form of nervousness and risk aversion. If it is the former, then professional support is required and always advocated. Your leadership role does not protect you from the normality of mental health challenges. You need to look after yourself.

If the prospect of uncertainty, complexity and ambiguity creates a low-grade anxiety, then start with the basics of a risk register and run a log of all the anticipated risks and proposed mitigations. As we discussed in the previous chapter, scenario planning is an effective way of managing 'what if?' When you have unresolved questions of 'what if' your brain will default to an obsessive looping of the question. Answer the question, and you calm the anxiety.

As we discussed in Chapter Four on mindsets, specifically the Agile Mindset, the shift from failure aversion to failure seeking is a game changer. At the risk of sounding like a broken record, we need to revisit shame again. Guy Winch (of Psychologist Today[2] says:

> 'Failing can elicit feelings such as disappointment, anger, frustration, sadness, regret and confusion that, while unpleasant, are usually not sufficient to trigger a full-blown fear of failure. Indeed, the term is somewhat of a misnomer because it is not failure per se that underlies the behaviour of people who have it. Rather, a fear of failure is essentially a fear of shame. People who have a fear of failure are motivated to avoid failing not because they cannot manage the basic emotions of disappointment, anger and frustration that accompany such experiences but because failing also makes them feel deep shame.'

If your discontent with leading in a 'messy' world is more about perfectionism, and we know messy is less than perfect, you do want to review the section on shame again. The desire to be a perfectionist is ultimately born of the fear of not being accepted by peers or loved. This one might need some external support by way of a counsellor or therapist. An adherence to perfectionism will absolutely be a barrier to leading in an agile way.

Shame separates and isolates. You will move further away from the change you need to lead to ensure that you do not feel deep shame. Shame (that drives fear of failure and perfectionist behaviours) thrives on silence. It's like an insidious cancer that eats away at the confidence of leaders. So, your change action here, while it may be deeply uncomfortable is profoundly effective.

Change Action #56: Seek out professional help to review your mental health. Consider this as important as your personal trainer for your physical health.

This chapter has covered six common obstacles faced by leaders in change:

- You won't feel safe
- You won't like your peers
- Imposter Syndrome
- You will still want control
- You want to be liked
- You don't like the messy

They are provided in this book in the spirit of full transparency. Doing the work on yourself to make you a better leader of change will not guarantee smooth passage.

This is the work of leading change, facing into obstacles and challenges and working through them regardless of how hard it gets.

Speaking of how hard it gets? It doesn't get harder than leading systemic change. The next chapter picks up on this. Refill your water, take seven deep breaths, and continue on.

Notes

1. https://hbr.org/2008/05/overcoming-imposter-syndrome#:~:text=Imposter%20syndrome%20can%20be%20defined,external%20proof%20of%20their%20competence
2. tps://www.psychologytoday.com/au/blog/the-squeaky-wheel/201306/10-signs-you-might-have-fear-failure

Chapter 7: The hardest changes you may lead

Oneka Jefferson-Cornelius, Michelle Redfern, and Kylie Lewis

You have a choice. You can continue to lead change that benefits your career, your organisation. Or you can use your privilege in broader context, namely transforming your organisation systemically. It will be exceptionally hard work and you will need stamina to do so.

This chapter presents three of the most difficult changes to make in organisations – anti-racism, achieving gender equality, and reversing climate change impacts. The first two – anti-racism and gender equality – typically fall under the 'Diversity and Inclusion' umbrella along with other criteria of diversity: age, sex, neurovariety, cognitive variety and cultural variations. I've chosen to focus on race and gender as I see these as urgent change agendas, and if addressed, can have a multiplier effect across all 'Diversity and Inclusion' areas of interest. If you can make changes in these two areas, you can make changes in others.

This deliberate choice of focus underscores the importance of having a clear change strategy for how you approach systemic change. You can't boil the ocean. If you're being strategic about what change you wish to lead, there will be winners and losers. Each decision you make has pros and cons in terms of speed of change, depth and breadth of change, personal and organisational reputation. Your choice to prioritise one agenda will create losers in other areas.

Whether you chose a de-sensitization strategy where you introduce an acceptable amount of the change and build tolerance so you can introduce more, whether you tackle the top and wait for the new values to trickle down into policy and process, whether you create a small passionate community which then mobilises others, there are trade-offs. And this is the conversation you need to be having with the person / people who have Diversity and Inclusion or Climate Crisis in their portfolio. If they can't have a conversation with you that clearly outlines their change strategy and their knowledge of the trade-offs, they will be unlikely to create effective change.

Additionally, a cautionary note. In all the three cases outlined above, much of the root cause of the poor 'current' state can be attributed with mankind's desire to have 'power over' and the desire to maintain capitalism as the dominant economic model. They are intrinsically interlinked and interwoven, and it does not matter from which country you are reading this book, you will find that the arena in which you have the opportunity to make change is isolated and not particularly crowded. You may feel very lonely in your commitment to lead change in these domains.

While I have been comfortable acknowledging how power plays out and actively engaging in different models of leading from a power perspective, I'm the first to say that recognising the role that pushing a capitalist agenda plays has been a bitter pill to swallow. But like the *power over – power with* continuum, there is a continuum of positions between communism and capitalism. And as noted in the beginning of this book any shift to the right improves your change leadership. Although perhaps in this case it is any shift to the left that reduces inequality?

The Pollyanna in me really wants to believe that you can meld capitalist models with social benefits, that entrepreneurship can drive community growth. And whether you are howling, scowling or cheering at this statement, I guess the main thing is that we continue to be attentive to the role that capitalism, the desire for 'ownership', and our inherent desire to have 'power over' shows up in our leadership, our decision-making and our sponsoring of change.

Recognising and acknowledging your role in perpetuating inequalities can raise feelings of shame which as we know from Chapter One can lead to outright denial, paralysis and avoidance of the topic. Who knows, perhaps this chapter was closed after the first few sentences?

If it hasn't, and you're still with me, I invite you to reread those pages on shame resilience and self-compassion, perhaps the full chapter on qualities. These qualities will help you stay with the voices that tell us a story of how to be a better leader of change in these domains in this chapter and help heal our organisations.

Some of you will have noted already there are still a few pages to go in this book. While I have made a commitment to making each of the chapters short, sharp and easily digestible, this one is not. It's too under-addressed compared to the other topics. The hardest changes to lead can't be dealt with an abbreviated version, and you may need to sit with some of the content for some time.

Onwards.

Anti-racism

I write this on the lands of the Wurundjeri Woi Wurrung people of the Kulin Nation as a white woman of extreme privilege.

Anti-racism as an organisational transformation agenda rose in 2020 on account of the visibility of the brutal murders of Black Americans George Floyd and

Breanna Taylor through social media channels. They were by no means the first, and certainly in Australia by the time the Black Lives Matter movement gained prominence in the US, the Guardian published a database that showed more than 400 Aboriginal and Islander people had died in custody since the Royal Commission into deaths in custody in 1991.[1]

'I can't breathe' were the last words of David Dungay Jr in 2015, while being held down by corrective officers in Long Bay Gaol, New South Wales.

With the rise of white attention to the inequity of Black Indigenous People of Colour (BIPOC) came visibility of many activists, writers, academics and spokespeople on the topic through social media initiatives such as 'pass the mic' and mainstream media interest. Books like White Fragility by Robin DiAngelo, How to be an Anti-Racist by Ibram X Kendi, and Me and White Supremacy by Layla F Saad hit best seller lists. Sales of books by Indigenous Australian writers also spiked [2]

Much of advocacy took the shape of Critical Race Theory which drew criticism for its divisiveness. 'Critical Race Theory provides the view that the law and legal institutions are inherently racist and that race itself, instead of being biologically grounded and natural, is a socially constructed concept that is used by white people to further their economic and political interests at the expense of people of colour'[3].

Any form of Critical Theory – whether it be in

management or in economics – operates to provide a reflexive investigation of the power structures in that field. The unearthing and illuminating of dominant power, which by its very essence means that that there are people, groups and organisations that are disempowered, creates friction.

One of the criticisms of the books listed above was that they created division when we should be seeking to harmonise (although this criticism most often came from senior white males who had the most to lose). The other criticism of critical race theory anti-racism efforts is it can be steeped in evangelistic Christian morality – racism is akin to original sin and must be outcast. Redemption is a form of moral progression and themes of confession, guilt and revelation ensue.

I found some of my most useful education from social justice educators and change-makers Thea Monyee [4] and EbonyJanice Moore[5] and their online lecture series. What I appreciated was they didn't shy away from exposition of power and white supremacy, but they did include an implicit focus on positive psychology which reduced the shame and created a space to keep moving and doing better. In response to criticisms of people who were uncomfortable with looking at the racism within, Monyee used the metaphor inspired by Black American novelist James Baldwin's metaphor of America and racism being like a burning house, 'When your house is on fire, how can you not have smoke in your lungs? You need to heal and get better'.

This recognition of racism within for white people can trigger intense shame. For most there is no greater insult than to be called a racist. And as we learnt in Chapter One shame shows up in heightened limbic systems prompting fight, flight, freeze responses. And we have seen this with white people facing up to in 2020.

Flight: White people saw the images, heard the stories and muted social media threads, turned the channel over and avoided conversations about the topic.

Fight: White people invested energy in denying they had privilege, that there were injustices, that they could have elements of racism within.

Freeze: White people acknowledged the issues and were paralysed. They were reluctant to say anything, do anything in case they said something or did something wrong.

From my perspective, the key to doing better from an anti-racism perspective is to build shame resilience. This enables you to lead change in this area. Leading change in this area is making your employees who are BIPOC feel safer, your customers who are BIPOC feel safer and creating products and services that are not 'white-centred'. Leading change in this area means proactively addressing the power imbalance around you in your organisation.

Organisational change interventions in anti-racism

To date, the popular inventions in organisations for

anti-racism consist of the 'day long' anti-racism workshop (also known derisively as 'sheep-dipping). We dip our people in an anti-racism workshop and they supposedly come out fixed. In a 1988 paper 'Developing Multi Cultural Organisations', authors Jackson and Holvino show that there has been limited success with individual consciousness raising and sustainable change requires large scale system intervention in the organisation.

Certainly, I know that in my 25-plus year career I have not seen people who are charged with increasing 'Diversity & Inclusion' engage with change practitioners, nor use strategic organisational change approaches. Jackson and Holvino note that traditional Organisational Development (OD) has not been effective in this area. They advocate the transitioning of an organisation though three stages of development as depicted in the diagram below.

The Multicultural Organizational Development model (Chaos Management Ltd, 2008) is made up of three 'phases'

MONOCULTURAL	
Exclusionary	**Passive**
Committed to the dominance, values and norms of one group. Actively excludes in its missions and practices those who are no members of the dominant group.	Actively or passively excludes those who are not members of the dominant group, includes others members of only if they 'fit' the dominant norm.
Values and promotes the dominant perspective of one group, culture, or style.	

TRANSITIONAL

Compliance	Positive action
Passibley committed to others without making major changes. Includes only a few members of other groups.	Committed to making a special effort to including others especially those in designated special 'classes'. Tolerates the differences that others bring.
Seeks to integrate others under systems that are created under dominant norms.	

MULTICULTURAL

Redefining	Multicultural
Actively works to expand its definition of diversity, inclusion and equity. Tries to examine and change practices that may act as barriers to non-dominating groups.	Actively includes a diversity of people representing different group styles and perspectives. Continuously learns and acts to make the systemic changes required to value, include and be fair to all kinds of people.
Values and integrates the perspectives of diverse identities, culture, styles and groups into the organization's work and systems.	

This can be a useful starting point to determine where you think your organisation is.[6]

With respect to the change strategy of 'forced change with consequence', a useful case study was recently provided by Target Chief Engagement Officer and Senior Vice President Laysha Ward where she outlines the eight-point framework for an Anti-Racist Business Strategy in the Harvard Business Review.[7]

Their foundation pillars are:

Purpose – why the change towards anti-racism matters to the company.

Perspectives – a deep and wide understanding of

what it is to experience organisational life as a BIPOC employee.

People – reviewing and changing people practices such as talent progression and recruiting.

Performance metrics – implementing the identification and tracking of diversity and inclusion metrics that are meaningful.

These are the minimum baseline elements to be activated. Then there is an additional four elements that each business leader is expected to consider and integrate.

Purchasing – increasing the amount of black owned businesses in your supply chain.

Philanthropy – committing to long-term, sustainable support of time, talent, financial resources and expertise.

Policy – examining your company's policies and practices with an anti-racist lens within the constraints of local legislation.

Place – focusing investments on the communities most impacted by racial inequity.

In the article Ward also cites Salesforce and Merck as large US corporations where the C-Suite is visibly and actively committing to developing anti-racist organisations.

Could your organisation be next? What will your role in that be?

I acknowledge I am on a big journey of learning and unlearning and this is not my story to share, nor my advice to give. While I have expertise in organisational change and transformation and am committed to doing better, I am part of the change that needs to happen. My house is on fire, I am clearing my lungs of the smoke. The one question that has stuck with me throughout 2020 (in recognition of how white my profession is) is, 'If we listened to the BIPOC change leaders in our organisations, would we hear something different about how to move forward and lead change in this domain? If my lungs are full of smoke, am I the right person to help you lead change in this domain?

For this reason, I would like to hand this section over to Oneka Jefferson-Cornelius, a Black leader of change, known for driving sustainable change and organisational effectiveness with a healing focus. She is the Executive Director of Convergence Solutions LLC – a consulting company that provides services in the domains of Talent, Organisational Effectiveness, OD, D&I and Change.

What do leaders need to know about leading change with respect to anti-racism'?

Oneka Jefferson-Cornelius

While all change occurs within the ecosystem of an organisation, it is important to understand and fully acknowledge how deep cultural change runs. We often note that culture within an organisation is described as 'the way we do things around here,' and so how we operate with respect to race in organisations must be considered a cultural imprint. So many of those 'things' that are done are unspoken, observed and perpetuated over time without asking...'Why?'

Like Jen, I've noted the absence of change strategists as full partners with Diversity and Equity Leaders, which I find interesting because there is no more significant change journey that any human being will go on outside of how they see themselves than how they see others.

Opportunities...and Obstacles

As with most cultural change initiatives, leading an anti-racism strategy is a marathon and not a sprint. There can be the inclination to hurry up and 'do something', but without clear understanding of how leaders and founders have built a business, select new and future leaders, build systems and decision-making mechanisms and most importantly, the work it will take to make the sustainable changes that will stick, so much of this hard (and necessary) work will not sustain.

We all know that change is hard: what we must reckon with is the importance of doing the internal, emotional and psychological work that is required FIRST. I often share with peers and clients that this type of work requires healing that must happen in/ for leaders FIRST. It requires the dismantling of often invisible belief systems about people groups, ethnicity, upbringing, exposure and if we're going to be honest, the trauma that people may have experienced that shapes their perspective about people who are different. These discussions require and demand sacred and (psychologically) safe spaces to be addressed.

Creating those spaces and the trust to use them correctly requires time, attention and intention. Diversity and equity transformations are heart issues, not merely policy or programming issues. If policy or programming were enough, it would have been resolved long ago. These transformations happen within oneself, then emerge and create new ways of thinking, doing and being. Heart-level transformation comes about through relationship.

In the absence of this, we create programs that don't help, we drive people with differing views away, and the necessary conversations for healing and change never take root or grow.

Change interventions that are effective

In order to lead transformation in the cultural domain of anti-racism there are three (3) areas to concentrate on.

Change Leadership

You're going to need to work earnestly with your leadership teams and your peers. It is critical to build trusted advisory relationships with those leaders who are willing to do the personal and internal work to be better people leaders. Leaders cast vision, they tell stories, they are examples. Do the deep work to understand your biases and what accountability looks like for you.

Leadership requires listening, and that will take time. Listening sessions, focus groups and debriefing of self-assessments can be an effective approach to building sacred spaces. I encourage deep introspection on these approaches with diversity and cultural change initiatives, because one should not expect people groups to be willing to vocalise and share (past or present) trauma in spaces that are not safe, and can result in retribution, attack, gaslighting or professional impacts, up to and including losing one's job and ability to provide.

Making your workplace safer for BIPOC or people who are not white to voice will also require a clear set of intentions with what to do with this type of information and how to leverage it wisely (and confidentially) as part of a holistic strategy.

Change Strategy and Vision

Strategic change, when done well, permeates the enterprise AND the environment. Create strategic change impacts that are measurable and inform leadership decision-making. Build it into annual business plans, people development, personal objectives, leadership assessments, cultural metrics, communication planning and more. If you are serious about leading change in this area, then anti-racism and diversity become integral to your north star, the guide by which all decisions, investments and people decisions are made and addressed.

Many ask who owns this strategy, it is NOT the change or diversity leader. It is the CEO, it is the business or function lead. Everyone and everything else align to this strategy because it is bigger than any one individual. Well-executed strategies can stand the test of time and remain intact, even as/when specific leaders move on, the strategy should be strong enough to remain.

Change Sustainability

Without a plan for what happens 'after', there will be no way to measure and ensure the changes needed become ingrained in how people lead, act and serve across the organisation. This will not be easy. This is where it becomes everyone's role/job/responsibility to keep going. It is hard and it is time-consuming, but it is worth it. Sustainability will create a focus across many dimensions, such as People, Process, Systems and Technology.

There can be bias in them all, and it will take time to identify, address, adjust and maintain them. Effective change sustainability will uncover issues no one ever addressed or corrected before, and will take time to ensure adequate and measurable accountability is possible.

Parting Wisdom

When talking with clients and partners about leading change, I always share the following:

'There is going to come a time in this process when it will be/feel bigger than you. You will realise that you've bitten off more than you can chew. You will make note of those peers, colleagues, clients and team members (at all levels) that may not be willing to make the heart and behaviour change(s) that are necessary. This is when the hard(est) decisions will need to be made. You will have to recognise that not everyone is willing to move forward. Some may self-select out and they will leave.

Others may hang in until things get tough and then will discover they aren't ready and will move on. Still others will adamantly disagree and will challenge you and you will have to stand firmly in the truth of what is right.

But, most importantly, there will be those who have been waiting for someone to 'call the question' and have the courage to move forward. These will be the people who will stand and do the work alongside you, or they will come forward and be ready to take it even farther than you imagined. Don't give up before they emerge.'

Change Action #57: Make a list of your peers that you know are committed to driving anti-racism in the organisation.

Change Action #58: Ask to see your organisation's anti-racism strategy to share with the peers identified in previous change action.

Change Action #59: Review your leadership performance metrics to understand how they can be adapted to include sustainable change metrics with respect to anti-racism.

Gender Equality

I'm one of the least qualified people to talk about gender equality. I was raised in a feminist household so I grew up relatively unaware of the challenges I should face or limiting beliefs about what 'girls' should do. I'm also white, well-educated and six-foot-tall (yes, there really is research that shows taller people are more likely to be promoted). It means I really haven't struggled with being heard, promoted or engaged because of my gender. At least I don't think I have.

That said, I have witnessed misogyny, sexual harassment and chauvinist behaviour in the workplace. So, I'm not ignorant to the problem, but I don't feel I have expertise in this and have been somewhat removed from the struggle. That's why I asked Michelle Redfern to contribute to this chapter. Michelle is the founder of Advancing Women in Business and Sport and a renowned researcher and advisor on gender diversity and inclusion, and an unabashed feminist who works with the C Suite on gender equality programs.

I asked Michelle to provide us with an overview of the current state of gender equality, what we could be achieving and what gets in the way. It's worth noting that for the purpose of this section we refer to two genders, male and female, and acknowledge that science now shows that while there are two sex forms there are multiple gender variants.

What do leaders need to know about leading change with respect to gender equality?

Michelle Redfern

Current state and future state

If we were just to look at the binary version of gender, the ideal future state would be 50/50. There will be equal numbers of men and women in workplaces, at every level across the world. We certainly want gender balance on Boards and in Executive teams, because there is irrefutable and contemporary evidence that gender diversity in the 'top teams' leads to better business outcomes.

And yet, we are a fair way away from that, with the delta being pretty big. Depending on which geography you're in or in which sector, or at what level of seniority, that delta can yawn very widely. For example, there are only 7.5% women CEOs in the S&P500 and only 5% women CEOs in the ASX200. The number of women on boards did rise significantly in recent years, however, it's now stagnating around the 29% to 30% mark. Executive leadership teams are dominated by men with only 32% of key management personnel roles held by women.

Now of course that is taking a very homogenous, binary view of equality in that it's the ratios of men to women. Once an intersectional lens is applied, there are more glaring inequities in terms of representation uncovered.

In Australia, there is a paucity of representation of those who identify as Aboriginal and Torres Strait Islander, people who identify as having a disability and those who have a culturally and/or linguistically diverse heritage, irrespective of gender. That's important to reflect on as there is no business anywhere in the world that doesn't have a consumer who belongs to one or more of these demographics.

Therefore, companies that are not yet gender balanced, not yet culturally diverse, not yet representative of society, are less likely to be representative of their consumers. Therefore, these companies do not necessarily create the goods, services and experiences that the people that buy their goods need or want.

The drivers of change

The drivers of change have shifted over the years. Once it was purely economic, and consultants and business leaders like me used to have to write business cases to support the changes required to achieve gender equality in the workplace.

The data about workplace gender composition has been available for many years, and rationally or economically it is a must-do. Just this year we have seen the world first research on how female CEOs and Board members boost companies market value.

The study, based on six years of Australian companies' gender reporting to the federal Workplace Gender Equality Agency, has established that companies who appointed a female CEO increased their market value by 5%. Similarly, the study found that increasing the number of female board members by 10% or more produces a 4.9% boost to a company's market value.

From an economic standpoint, when women participate more in the workforce, they earn more, and as a result they spend more.

We all know what the knock-on effect is from a rise in consumer spending. Research by Femeconomy has proven that women in heterosexual family units influence between 75% and 80% of the family household spending.

So, this links back to one of the reasons why organisations must be more intentional about increasing the representation of women at the top, particularly in the roles that drive product development, innovation and focus on the customer/ consumer.

And yet, we have not seen the business case drive improvement, as evidenced by the low level of maturity of the current state. The conversation is evolving to one about social justice. Creating gender balanced, inclusive workplaces is simply the right thing to do. Conversations at Board and executive levels focus more on how does the company hold up itself up to external scrutiny?

The change interventions

Typically, organisations buy packages from consultants where they 'sheep-dip' everyone through the same unconscious bias program. It's really ineffective. Successful change comes through large scale systemic behaviour change programs which start at the top.

The leaders at the top must be all in to make this work. It's not the role of the person with D&I in their title. Ideally, everyone has D&I in the role descriptor!

At the end of the day, the organisation's strategy, the financial strategy, the strategy for growth, the strategy for, 'This is what we do in this business', happens at the Board and at the Executive table, and unless those two sets of stakeholders are fully onboard, it's a tough road.

The road forward starts with a very personal examination by leadership of what their brutal truths are. The very basic brutal truths that organisations must confront are:

- What are the numbers of women at every level in your organisation?
- What is the lived experience for women in your organisation?

One of my peers has a great question to the leaders she works with: Would you be comfortable with your mother, your best friend, your sister, your daughter or your wife working in this company? When the leadership has recognised and acknowledged the brutal truths, they are in a position to go through and sponsor a constant flow of new information, resources, tools and experts on the topic.

And it also comes through structural change – this is why we have debate around universal childcare and why access to childcare is so important. When you have a courageous government or an organisation that makes that happen, you create opportunities for women to work.

Barriers to change

Most of the barriers to change are personal.

To discover at a very senior leadership level that you are not skilled or knowledgeable in a particular domain can be very humbling or humiliating.

That humiliation can lead to a desire to bluff and not listen to others. You've got to learn to sit in the uncomfortable knowledge that you're not an expert – and develop a tolerance for discomfort.

When leaders undertake the beginning of a gender equality change program, they're about to undertake a program of change to create a more inclusive workplace. The very first thing to be on the alert for is the person who says, 'Yep. Yep. I know all about this.'

The reality is, if that person did know all about 'this', they (and arguably the organisation) would not be in the low level of maturity that they are. This type can be challenging; however, one of the ways to engage the 'yeppers' as I call them, is to ask them to share their wisdom, the techniques and to take the lead on aspects of the change program.

The second thing to be on the lookout for are the leaders who are very experienced, very respected, who have delivered outstanding results and have a proven track record. Because they are the ones we need to be most kind and compassionate to. They now find that they are in a position of low power, low knowledge, and they've got to admit that they are there.

Irrespective of the types of personalities or the maturity of the organisation or the leaders, I find it useful to frame this change with this narrative:

> You are building a set of 21st century leadership skills.
>
> Inclusion, diversity and belonging are no longer 'nice to have'.
>
> You are demonstrating to your organisation and its stakeholders that you are serious about creating and sustaining a high-performance organisation.
>
> You are more likely to enjoy and be fulfilled in your role as a result of this change.

The way forward

The way forward is challenging as it means deep introspection. You need to know who you are and what you stand for. This means getting in touch with your own values and acknowledging your own mindsets about women, work and leadership. You will have blind spots, we all do!

Understand that it is your responsibility to educate yourself about the barriers that women and other under-represented people face. It is not their responsibility to educate you.

Listen with the mindset to learn about the lived experience of women. That means taking the time to deliberately engage with women in your workplace to understand the good, the bad and the ugly.

We want you to be an active ally, please. This means actively involving yourself in initiatives and activities aimed at addressing gender inequality in your workplace. Offer help, do not wait to be asked. Be an upstander, not a bystander.

Change Action #60: Speak up loudly the minute you see sexism, harassment or inequality in the workplace.

Change Action #61: Ask yourself – would I want my mother, my best friend, my sister, my daughter or my wife working in this company.

Change Action #62: Make a public statement (in a team meeting, or on your enterprise social network) of your intent to elevate gender equality in your organisation.

Climate crisis

I personally have been in a shame response on reversing climate change impacts for many years. I feel it's futile, it's too overwhelming, and take some solace in sorting the recyclables the best way I can, turning off lights, sweating it out in summer a little longer before turning on the air-conditioner, shivering in winter before turning on the heater. But that's about it, to be honest.

It would be hypocritical for me to tell you how to lead change in this domain, because I am struggling with it. Its why I am very grateful to Kylie Lewis to talk us through this topic. Kylie is leadership developer, a qualified facilitator of Dr Brene Brown's work on courage, vulnerability, shame and resilience, and founder of Of Kin, a training organisation specialising in building brave leaders and courageous cultures. Having undertaken Climate Reality training with former Vice President Al Gore's Climate Reality Project, she is committed to assisting others to reverse climate change impacts in organisations and communities.

What do leaders need to know about leading change with respect to the climate crisis?

Kylie Lewis

Current State

> 'We are dependent on the natural world for every breath of air we take and every mouthful of food we eat. But it's even more that that we are also dependent on it for our sanity and sense of proportion'

> Sir David Attenborough

In Australia, we welcomed 2020, the most important decade for addressing the climate crisis, on fire. Apocalyptic scenes of our country folk huddled on beaches under literal burnt orange skies, choking on smoke, terrified of the loss of life and livelihoods, with a soundtrack of three billion animals burning alive. Rainforests we believed could never fall victim to bushfires burned for the first time. Veteran firefighters reported there had never been fire events of this magnitude or intensity in living memory.

Regarding metrics that matter, at the time of writing we have 11 years, 9 months left before global temperatures reach the 1.5 – 2 degrees Celsius threshold noted in the Paris Agreement, although change is happening faster than predicted [8].

The disruption to your family, your leadership, your business, your industry, your employees and your clients brought by COVID19 is a preview of the disruption that lays ahead. Climate change, public health and social justice are all interconnected.

We already see that the most disadvantaged communities are the most effected by poor air quality, polluted water ways and extreme weather events. An overheated planet makes extreme weather events more frequent, bringing with them increases in diseases, food insecurity and population displacement. Scientists are worried about not only rising sea levels on our shores, but the unknown bacteria thawing in our ice masses.

You are fully dependent on this planet for every single thing you have in your life Every. Single. Thing. The food you eat, the water you drink, the air you breath to stay alive. The desk you work on, the house you live in, the job you toil at. Without the regeneration and stability of our literal life support system, everything fails.

But whether we acknowledge it or not, we are all now living in a state of a climate emergency, regardless of if your elected officials have declared it so. Climate and health scientists have been telling us for decades that the more we destroy our natural environment, the sicker we are.

The more we extract from it, chop it down and clear it, build over it, bury waste back into it, or ignore it, the more precarious our own existence is. The less time we spend in nature, the more disconnected we are from our own.

Future State

'The most important question facing humanity is this: Can we reach global empathy in time to avoid the collapse of civilization and save the Earth?'

Jeremy Rifkin, The Empathic Civilization: The Race to Global Consciousness in A world in Crisis.

Our future depends on what we choose to do right now. Scientists believe we can maintain our existence, if we do not pander to wilful blindness or 'predatory delay' which is defined as 'the blocking or slowing of needed change, in order to make money off unsustainable, unjust systems in the meantime. [9].

Lloyd Alter, design editor of online magazine Tree Hugger, explains: 'It is not delay from the absence of action, but delay as a plan of action – a way of keeping things the way they are for the people who are benefiting now, at the expense of the next and future generations.'

Ultimately, the climate crisis is a leadership crisis, where the stakes are beyond what we feel comfortable acknowledging. Leadership, however, is always about doing what is right over what is fun, fast or easy.

It is about what Jim Collins calls The Stockdale Paradox: 'Maintaining unwavering faith that you can and will prevail in the end, regardless of the difficulties, and at the same time, have the discipline to confront the most brutal facts of your current reality, whatever they might be.'

Barriers to Change

The brutal facts are that addressing the climate crisis is a change management initiative beyond the scale of anything humanity has ever had to enact. Like any change initiative, we must tackle both the personal stories and the public barriers to change. Some of the most common personal narratives we hear are:

- I have to do it all and do it all perfectly.
- The problem is beyond help so why bother?
- It's too big and too hard for me as one person to influence.
- It's something future generations will fix.
- It's something technology will fix.
- It's not that bad.
- I don't know how.
- I don't have time.
- I'm exhausted.

To which I call on the wisdom of Arthur Ashe, the first Black American tennis player to play in the Davis Cup. He invites us to 'Start where you are. Use what you have. Do what you can.' As zero-waste activist Anne Marie Bonneau says, 'We don't need a handful of people doing zero waste perfectly. We need millions of people doing it imperfectly.'

Some of the most common public discourse to systems change include:

- It will cost jobs.
- We've got time so change can wait.
- It's someone else's problem to fix.
- We don't contribute significantly to the problem.
- There are no viable, affordable alternatives.
- It's the government's job to fix.
- It's industry's job to fix.

To which I say, we can't afford to stay the same; we can afford to change if we have the political will (rapid COVID relief funding proved this); we are globally interdependent and reliant on each other for survival; renewable energy is now cheaper to build, maintain and consume than fossil fuels; a green and blue economy is the one of the few growth industries we have; and we need both government (local, state and federal) and industry to fix it.

What a leader can do

> 'You cannot get through a single day without having an impact on the world around you. What you do makes a difference, and you have to decide what kind of difference you want to make.'

> Jane Goodall

You first need to determine how you will integrate climate leadership into your organisation's daily, weekly, monthly, yearly practices? How will you and your organisation lead on climate?

Many organisations are recruiting now and appointing senior roles in Climate Change policy, but to wait for this is another form of resistance to change. There are simple things you can do immediately and build a groundswell within your organisation.

Start with the following three change actions to build momentum. And then find another three. And then another three. You lead by small steps, taken daily.

Change Action #63: Initiate uncomfortable conversations about the future of the organisation, your community, your staff, and your families if you continue business as usual.

Change Action #64: Reduce your business' carbon output and build carbon offsetting into your budgets and pricing.

Change Action #65: Put your support behind brokering

a bulk energy deal for your staff at home.

In change we often look for the rational and emotional reasons for change.

The three areas we've just been through are incredibly difficult to face into as any resistance you show to these topics exists from a long history of conditioning and systemic oppression.

The rational reason for embracing diversity and inclusion is clear – as Michelle pointed out in her essay on gender diversity, the financial ROI has always been there for gender equality. Your customers and clients are diverse. We trade globally.

The science on renewable resources or the lack of is abundantly clear. You cannot get any more rational.

If you are choosing not to champion change for gender equality or anti-racism, or climate crisis, it can only be an emotional resistance – perhaps shame has taken hold.

Perhaps on some level you don't believe in equality, and do not wish to relinquish the power you currently hold. This goes for women as well as men.

This realisation may come as a bit of a gut punch for a few of you, an insight that is difficult to swallow given how attached we are to thinking we are 'good and nice' people.

Sit with it. We live in a world of paradox. It is possible to be 'good and nice' and be inherently bigoted in some way.

Ultimately, you are in an incredibly privileged position of power. What could be more 'good or nice', than to use that position for systemic and serious change?

Notes

1. https://www.theguardian.com/australia-news/2019/aug/23/indigenous-deaths-in-custody-worsen-over-year-of-tracking-by-deaths-inside-project
2. https://www.abc.net.au/news/2020-06-19/bookshop-surge-in-race-indigenous-book-titles/12363728
3. https://www.britannica.com/topic/critical-race-theory
4. https://www.theamonyee.com/
5. https://ebonyjanice.com/
6. With thanks to Preston V. L. Lindsay of The Lindsay Group, https://www.thelindsaygroup.co/ for sharing the paper as part of his anti-racist OCM toolkit.
7. https://hbr.org/2020/11/what-an-anti-racist-business-strategy-looks-like
8. https://www.theguardian.com/environment/2021/jan/25/global-ice-loss-accelerating-at-record-rate-study-finds
9. https://www.treehugger.com/jargon-watch-predatory-delay-4852853

Chapter 8: To conclude, or perhaps begin?

We will not go back to normal, normal never was. Our pre-Corona existence was not normal, other than we normalized greed, inequity, exhaustion, depletion, extraction, disconnection, confusion, rage, hoarding, hate, and lack. We should not long to return, my friends, we are being given the opportunity to stitch a new garment, one that fits all of humanity and nature.

Sonya Renee Taylor

These words from the poet and author Sonya Renee Taylor ricocheted around the world when shared on social media. There were many who, in the midst of the chaos of 2020, heard a quiet voice from within that said 'returning to normal' was not an option.

That this was an opportunity to work in different ways, relate in different ways, to lead in different ways.

There was ample evidence to suggest that 'normal' was not good.

This book has offered you 33 topics to seek to 'shift the dial' and make incremental changes in the way you lead that build to major transformative change.

- Emotional intelligence
- Strengths
- SCARF ™
- Relationship to power
- Relationship to shame
- Trust
- Collaboration
- Social Stakeholders
- Communication
- Influence
- Exploratory Leadership
- Beginners Mindset
- Done is better than perfect
- Releasing command and control
- Failure seeking
- Empathy
- Vulnerability
- Courage
- Curiosity
- Mindful Self-compassion

- Data informed decision making
- Uncertainty reduction
- Strategic forecasting
- Keeping calm
- You won't feel safe
- You won't like your peers
- Imposter Syndrome
- You will still want control
- You want to be liked
- You don't like the messy
- Anti-racism
- Gender-equality
- Climate-crisis

From this are 65 small actions that you can try over the next weeks to change how you lead. Success will be born of repetition. They are captured in the list over page for ease of access.

Consider it your own private leadership development program, although if your organisation wants to talk to me about using it for company at large I'm very happy to discuss!

So, the question I pose to you, dear leader, is if not now, then when?

When will you chose to shift the dial, to change

the way you lead to 'stitch this new garment' that will cloak the new organisational form?

You can expect continued disruption.

The storm is the norm.

Change. Leader.

List of Change Actions by Chapter

CHAPTER 1: KNOW THYSELF

Change Action #1: Sponsor the introduction of an organisational mindfulness program.

Change Action #2: Speak with a counsellor, coach or therapist about your emotional capacity to lead.

Change Action #3: Do a SCARF self-assessment to understand your biases and check with your team on their biases – are they in alignment?

Change Action #4: Review your leadership communications – are they equally weighted in effort to reduce threat to all five elements?

Change Action #5: Re-take your strengths assessment.

Change Action #6: Review the next three months. How can you marshal and maximise the strengths that will set you up for navigating continuing uncertainty?

Change Action #7: Reach out to each of your direct reports and provide some feedback on the strengths you have observed in 2020.

Change Action #8: Audit your sources of power. If you look to peers who seem to be navigating the disruptiveness well, are they using power with or new power?

Change Action #9: Find a new journal that you can dedicate to exploring thoughts about shame. When you catch yourself in a moment of shame, write down what caused it, and what you think you would say to your best friend if they told you about it.

CHAPTER 2: COLLABORATING AND COMMUNICATING THROUGH DISRUPTIVE CHANGE

Change Action #10: Conduct a BRAVING INVENTORY – how do you stack up?

Change Action #11: Map your social stakeholder network – who is missing?

Change Action #12: Note the communities you have access to that you could use to identify missing collaborative partners.

Change Action #13: Draw up the axis of collaborative potential and note one stakeholder in each grid to test the approaches.

Change Action #14: Create a message platform for the next three months.

Change Action #15: Review the think / act / do

framework with a change that is immediately important to you.

Change Action #16: Use an upcoming change that you are sponsoring and review your power of influence using Aristotles' Pathos, Ethos and Logos.

Change Action #17: Use an upcoming conversation that you need to influence and map out the key components of the Conversations of Influence model

CHAPTER 3: MINDSETS MATTER

Change Action #18: Reflect on your childhood explorations; if there was one element of how you used to explore as a child that you could bring forward tomorrow, what would it be?

Change Action #19: Make a list of explorers that you admire. What of their behaviours could you model yourself on?

Change Action #20: Enrol in an art class and spend some time being creative

Change Action #21: Create a team challenge to catch each other using sentences that could benefit from the word 'yet'. Keep a tally and reward the person who caught the most in a specific time frame.

Change Action #22: Consider the next change you need to deliver as a leader. What would the MVP look like?

Change Action #23: Define what you need to feel comfortable releasing a new policy, process, product or service in your business.

Change Action 24: Start your meetings with your

team by declaring the intent of what you want to do.

Change Action #25: Review the capability program with your direct reports. What learning and development needs to happen for you to loosen your grip?

Change Action #26: Write down the last three failures that occurred under your leadership. Reflect on to what extent they damaged your brand and value. Is there evidence that they did? Or did it lead to a more innovative outcome?

Change Action #27: Investigate your organisational learning processes and platforms. Do they need to improve to support a culture of failure seeking?

CHAPTER 4: QUALITIES OF LEADERS FOR THE FUTURE

Change Action #28: Note three people in your professional orbit that you could safely be a little more open with about your feelings.

Change Action #29: Review the week ahead. Where is there opportunity to be a little more vulnerable in your communication?

Change Action #30: End of week huddle: ask everyone to share a professional high and low and focus on responding with empathy.

Change Action #31: Go out for a coffee by yourself and spend time watching people and trying to imagine what is going on in their world.

Change Action #32: Notice when you move to judgment and the time it takes to do so.

Change Action #33: Create 30 minutes in your week to explore something without an agenda.

Change Action #34: Seek surprise – ask one of your employees or colleagues to tell you something you don't know that you should know.

Change Action #35: Identify one domain where you could be 10% braver and take action.

Change Action #36: Reflect on who demonstrates courage in your immediate circles. Is it bravery as usual or a leaping from a burning platform kind of courage?

Change Action #37: Draft a supportive and encouraging note to yourself on how you are handling the current challenges. Write it as if you were writing to your best friend.

Change Action #38: Download Insight Timer app on your phone and find a loving kindness meditation to listen to.

CHAPTER 5: LEADING THROUGH UNCERTAINTY

Change Action #39: Review the extent to which you are using data in your decision- making. Is it operational data to exploit efficiency? Is it strategic to explore opportunities?

Change Action #40: Catalogue the sources of data you currently use in your decision- making. Where are there gaps?

Change Action #41: Review your leadership communications for the week ahead. What are the stability messages in them?

Change Action #42: Review your leadership

communications for the quarter ahead. How can you increase the frequency and 'slice' the information further? What are the opportunities for sense-making?

Change Action #43: Identify a grounding technique that works for you and practice daily.

Change Action #44: At the end of each week, write five 'thank-you' notes and send to people in your organisation.

Change Action #45: Clear space in your diary to have a session with a direct report with no agenda, just to listen to their thoughts.

Change Action #46: Identify three things that have stayed the same over the last 18 months.

Change Action #47: Stop and take seven breaths.

Change Action #48: Stop and drink a glass of water.

CHAPTER 6: OBSTACLES YOU WILL FACE

Change Actions #49: Identify your safety net. Pause and do a 360-degree review; what are the elements and who are the people who make you feel safer?

Change Action #50: Conduct a strength spotting conversation with someone you don't think highly of.

Change Action #51: Have a conversation with yourself from the perspective of your best friend. What would they advise you on your feelings of unworthiness?

Change Action #52: Use 'I intend to...' to turn passive followers into active leaders.

Change Action #53: Resist the urge to provide solutions – sit in the uncertainty a little longer.

Change Action #54: Specify goals, not methods.

Change Action #55: Question your reluctance to act. To what extent is it based on a need for people to like you?

Change Action #56: Seek out professional help to review your mental health. Consider this as important as your personal trainer for your physical health.

CHAPTER 7: THE HARDEST CHANGES YOU MAY LEAD

Change Action #57: Make a list of your peers that you know are committed to driving anti-racism in the organisation.

Change Action #58: Ask to see your organisation's anti-racism strategy to share with the peers identified in previous change action.

Change Action #59: Review your leadership performance metrics to understand how they can be adapted to include sustainable change metrics with respect to anti-racism.

Change Action #60: Speak up loudly the minute you see sexism, harassment or inequality in the workplace.

Change Action #61: Ask yourself – would I want my mother, my best friend, my sister, my daughter or my wife working in this company.

Change Action #62: Make a public statement (in a

team meeting, or on your enterprise social network) of your intent to elevate gender equality in your organisation.

Change Action #63: Initiate uncomfortable conversations about the future of the organisation, your community, your staff, and your families if you continue business as usual.

Change Action #64: Reduce your business's carbon output and build carbon offsetting into your budgets and pricing.

Change Action #65: Put your support behind brokering a bulk energy deal for your staff at home.

Leaders Bookshelf

What follows is a list of books you should have on your nightstand or office bookshelf to be reading or to reread. Not all of these have been referenced in this book, but they all set you up well to lead through disruptive change.

Brown, B. (2018). *Dare to lead*. London: Vermilion.

Carnegie, D. (1964). *How to win friends and influence people*. New York: Simon and Schuster,

Collins, J., & Lazier, B. (2020). *Beyond entrepreneurship 2.0*, Random House Business

Dweck, C. S. (2006). *Mindset: The new psychology of success*. New York: Random House.

Ferguson, K., & Fox, C. (2018). *Women Kind: Unlocking the power of women supporting women*. Murdoch books.

Gates, B. (2021). *How to avoid a climate disaster: The solutions we have and the breakthroughs we need*. Alfred A Knopfs.

Goleman, D. (2002). *Primal leadership: Realizing the power of emotional intelligence*. Boston, Mass: Harvard Business School Press.

Heath, C., & Heath, D. (2011). *Switch: How to change*

things when change is hard. Waterville, Me: Thorndike Press.

Heimans, J., & Timms, H. (2019). *New Power: How anyone can persuade, mobilise and succeed in our chaotic and connected age*. New York: Anchor Books.

Kelly, L., Medina, C., & Cameron, D. (2014). Rebels at work. O'Reilly Media.

Lancaster, C. (2020). *Reimagine change, escape change fatigue, build resilience and awaken your creative brilliance*. Grammar Factory.

Marquet, L. D. (2015). *Turn the ship around*! Portfolio Penguin.

Marquet, L. D. (2020). *Leadership is language*. Portfolio Penguin.

Pink, D. H. (2009). Drive: *The surprising truth about what motivates us*. New York: Riverhead Books.

Ries, E. (2011). The *lean start-up*: *How today's entrepreneurs use continuous innovation to create radically successful businesses*. New York: Crown Business.

Ross, L. (2017). *Hacking for agile change: With an agile mindset, behaviours and practices*. (Paperback)

Saad, L. (2020). *Me and White Supremacy*: *How to recognise your privilege, combat racism and change the world*. King of Prussia, PA: Quercus.

Scott, K. (2019). *Radical candor: How to get what you want by saying what you mean*. London: Pan Books.

Semler, *R*. (1993). *Maverick*: *The success story behind the world's most unusual workplace*. New York, NY: Warner Books.

Shonstrom, E. (2015). *Wild curiosity: How to unleash creativity and encourage lifelong wondering*. Lanham, MD: Rowman and Littlefield.

Map your change actions

Why not use this map to do an intuitive assessment of where you are at today (or contact me for a downloadable version). Then, put the Change Actions into play on a regular basis and reassess in three months to see how much you have changed.

References

Amabile, T. M., & Kramer, S. J. (2011). The power of small wins. *Harvard Business Review*, 89(5).

Aristotle. *Rhetoric*. (Translated W. Rhys Roberts). The Internet Classics Archive.

Brown, B. (2018). *Dare to lead*. London: Vermilion.

Buckingham, M., & Clifton, D. O. (2001). *Now, discover your strengths*. New York: Free Press.

Collins, J., & Lazier, B. (2021). *Beyond entrepreneurship 2.0*. Cornerstone Digital.

Conner, D. (1993). *Managing at the speed of change: How resilient managers succeed and prosper where others fail*. New York: Villard Books.

Edelman Trust Barometer (2021). https://www.edelman.com/trust/2021-trust-barometer

Edmundson, A. C. (2011). Strategies for learning from failure. *Harvard Business Review*, 89(4), 48–55.

Edmondson, A. C., & Lei, Z. (2014) Psychological safety: The history, renaissance, and future of an interpersonal construct. *Annual Review of Organisational Psychology and Organisational Behavior*, 1, 23–43.

Feltman. C. (2008). *The thin book of trust: An essential primer for building trust at work.* Thin Book Publishing.

French Jr., J. R. P., & Raven, B. H. (1959). The bases of social power. In D. Cartwright (Ed.), *Studies in social power* (pp. 150–167). Ann Arbor, MI: Institute for Social Research.

Goleman, D. (1995). *Emotional intelligence.* New York: Bantam Books, Inc.

Heath, C., & Heath, D. (2007). *Made to stick: Why some ideas survive, and others die.* Chicago, New York: Random House.

Himmelman, A. T. (January 2002). *Collaboration for a change: Definitions, decision-making models, roles, and collaboration process guide.* Minneapolis, MN: Himmelman Consulting.

Heimann, J., & Timms, H. B. (2019). *New Power: How anyone can persuade, mobilise and success in our chaotic and connected age.* New York: Anchor Books.

Jackson, B.W. and Holvino, E. 1988. Developing Multicultural Organizations. *The Journal of Religion and the Applied Behavioral Sciences,* 9 (2): 14-19

Le Breton, D. (1996). *Adventure the passion of detours.* Editions Autremont

Marquet, L. D. (2015). *Turn the ship around!* Portfolio Penguin.

McClelland, D. C. (1987). *Human motivation.* New York: University of Cambridge.

Neff, K. D., & Germer, C. (2017). Self-Compassion and psychological wellbeing. In J. Doty (Ed.), *Oxford handbook of compassion science* Chap. 27. Oxford, UK: Oxford University Press.

Peterson, C., & Seligman, M. (2004) *Character strength and virtues handbook* (CSV).

Rock, D. (2008) SCARF: A brain-based model for collaborating with and influencing others. *NeuroLeadership Journal*, 1(1), 44.

Ross, L. (2017). *Hacking for agile change: With an agile mindset, behaviours and practices.* (Paperback)

Ryan, M. K., & Haslam, S. A. (9 February 2005). The Glass Cliff: Evidence that women are over-represented in precarious leadership positions. *British Journal of Management*, 16(2): 81–90.

Salovey, P., & Mayer, J. D. (1990). Emotional intelligence. *Imagination, Cognition, and Personality*, 9: 185–211.

Schumpeter, J. A. (2008). *Capitalism, socialism, and democracy.* HarperCollins.

Shonstrom, E. (2016). *Wild curiosity: How to unleash creativity and encourage lifelong wondering.* Lanham, MD: Rowman & Littlefield.

Young, V. (2011). *The secret thoughts of successful women: Why capable people suffer from imposter syndrome and how to thrive in spite of it.* New York: Crown Business.

ADDITIONAL WEB RESOURCES

Brown, B. (2009). The power of vulnerability. TEDx Talk. https://www.ted.com/talks/brene_brown_the_power_of_vulnerability/transcript?language=en

Edelman Trust Barometer (2021). https://www.edelman.com/trust/2021-trust-barometer

Frahm, J (2019) Helen Bevan – the long-time leader of change within the UK's NHS https://drjenfrahm.com/helen-bevan-nhs/

Frahm, J (2020) Exploratory Leadership and Big

Bounds. https://drjenfrahm.com/exploratory-leadership-and-big-bounds/

Frahm, J (2021) Podcast interview with Stewart Bird https://drjenfrahm.com/leading-change-with-data/

Schillinger, C (2014) https://weneedsocial.com/blog/2014/10/2/forget-social-networks-think-social-impact

Zak, P. J https://hbr.org/2017/01/the-neuroscience-of-trust

About the Author

DR JEN FRAHM is a global expert on organisational change and transformation and an executive coach. Jen is a tamer of ambiguity, teller of truths and solver of problems. A sought-after speaker, she is known for being at the frontier of business agility.

She is also the co-founder of The Agile Change Leadership Institute, author of Conversations of Change: A guide to workplace change (2017), and co-author of The Agile Change Playbook (2020). She is available to speak at your organisation, conference or assist in design and delivery of organisational change.

Previously an academic, Jen's research interests cover organisational theory, organisational change, organisational communication, and qualitative research methods. She has lectured in undergrad, postgrad and executive programs in leadership, organisational behaviour, project management, entrepreneurship, innovation, and government / business relations.

She has designed and delivered change across multiple industries and professions, from wine sales to wedding dresses, veterinary products to energy retailers, nuns and engineers, big banks, small IT companies, publicly listed, privately owned and non-profit organisations, and across 28 countries.